GREYS' GHOSTS:

MEN OF THE SCOTS GREYS
AT WATERLOO 1815

GREYS' GHOSTS

Men of the Scots Greys at Waterloo 1815

by

Stuart Mellor

© Stuart Mellor and Savannah Publications
First published 2012
All rights reserved. No part of this publication may be reproduced in any form without permission

Published by Savannah Publications
90 Dartmouth Road, Forest Hill, London SE23 3HZ, UK
British Library Cataloguing in Publication Data

A CIP catalogue record is available from the British Library
ISBN 1 902366 52 2
EAN 9781902366524

Published in the UK by Lightning Source
Front Cover: From a painting by Lynne Meakin

Contents

The spoils of war, the Eagle of the French 45th, for whose capture the Scots Greys paid a high price

Dedicated to the British soldiers
whose sacrifice and bravery enables
Britain to enjoy freedom

Foreword

The Royal Scots Dragoon Guards are Scotland's senior regiment and her only Regular Cavalry. Our history and traditions – most notable among them the charge of the Royal Scots Greys at Waterloo – are still held in high regard by the Regiment, with Waterloo Day being celebrated on 18 June every year wherever the Regiment happens to be serving. Whenever duties permit, the opportunity may also be taken to join with the successor regiments of the 1st Dragoons and 6th Dragoons to revive past camaraderie and, on occasion, to re-enact the famous Union Brigade 'leap', although less so now that modern health and safety regulations have (fortunately) imposed a modicum of restraint on would-be participants!

The Regiment's museum, which is housed in Edinburgh Castle and which enjoys an annual visitor total of 430,000, houses many artefacts relating to the Greys' exploits at Waterloo including medals, weapons and other accoutrements. The account of that great battle is explained in great detail and takes pride of place among the many other battle honours of the current Regiment and its antecedents.

July 2011 has seen the 40th Anniversary of the formation of the Royal Scots Dragoon Guards. The successor to three famous regiments – the 3rd Dragoon Guards, the 6th Dragoon Guards (Carabiniers) and the Royal Scots Greys (2nd Dragoons) – today's Regiment embodies all the fighting spirit, flair and panache of its famous forebears. During its recent history the Regiment has served on operations in Northern Ireland, Belize, the Balkans, Kuwait, Iraq and Afghanistan. Although it retains the tradition, the Regiment is no longer mounted on its famous grey horses, although the role remains that of mounted close combat. Over the years the Regiment has crewed a variety of platforms, both wheeled and tracked, with which to engage its enemies. Presently based in Fallingbostel, Northern Germany, the Regiment has recently returned from a gruelling tour of Helmand Province in Southern Afghanistan. In common with other regiments, the Royal Scots Dragoon Guards set up its own charitable appeal, 'Caring For Courage' to raise money for those wounded on all operations and the families of those killed; for it will always be to the regimental family that those in dire need will turn. The response from both the wider regimental family and the public has been magnificent.

As Colonel of the Royal Scots Dragoon Guards, I am profoundly grateful to Stuart Mellor for writing this book, which has added a new dimension to the wealth of information that exists surrounding the battle. For us as a Regiment it is even more poignant as we begin to learn more about our forebears and the sort of people they were. Sadly, there were no charities to meet their immediate needs following the battle and the Regiment is therefore even more indebted to the Author for offering all the royalties from this publication to the Caring For Courage Fund. As you read this book, it is hard not to hear the jangle of harness, the quiet snorting of horses and to sense the discipline of the troop. The 'Greys' Ghosts' would have approved.

Brigadier Simon Allen
Colonel, Royal Scots Dragoon Guards
December 2011

Acknowledgements

The production of this work on the Scots Greys at Waterloo would not have been possible without the assistance of friends and military enthusiasts. Initially one of my fears was that the list of contributors would exceed the number of pages in the text. This, I am relieved to state, has not been the case.

My interest in the Scots Greys began 30 years ago when I became a collector of military medals. However, it was the book by Alan Lagden and John Sly, *The 2/73rd Regiment at Waterloo* (1998), which stimulated my thoughts to consider writing a similar one on the 2nd Dragoons, later known as the Scots Greys. The idea was discussed with another fellow medal collector, Alan Harrison, and, with his encouragement and support, I decided to go ahead with this project.

The main objective was to rectify the lack of information on the men who charged with the Scots Greys at Waterloo. My first hurdle was to overcome my inexperience in researching material at the National Archives. This was principally solved by my introduction to Mr Peter John who is an accomplished and most helpful military researcher. He has been mainly responsible for the acquisition of information, including obtaining a copy of the Waterloo period muster rolls for the Regiment. I am most grateful to him for his effort and patience.

Any doubts I had about continuing this work were soon dismissed by the further assistance and support from the following, in no order of merit: Alan Lagden, Ian Laidler, Bob Green, Alan Harrison, Barry Gregson, Clifford Mansfield, Dr John M Cruickshank, Mick Crumplin FRCS, Martyn Lovell FRCS, David Ingham, Chris Mercer, David McCarthy, Robin Scott-Smith, Ian Kilgour, Robert Gottlieb, John Foreman, David Miles and Nimrod Dix of Dix Noonan Webb.

To those whom I have inadvertently omitted from the above list, I give my sincere apologies. However a special mention must be given to Major R Maclean of the Royal Scots Dragoon Guards for his continued support and contribution to this work.

I would like to express my appreciation to Geoff Bailey and Jean Jamieson of the Falkirk Museum for their excellent and invaluable contribution to the chapter 'The Falkirk Dozen'. I would also like to acknowledge Manchester Art Gallery and its staff for enabling me to obtain a copy of Charles Ewart's portrait. Similarly, thank you to George Duckett of Thomas Del Mar Ltd for permission to include Lieutenant Stupart's portrait from their auction catalogue.

Lynne Meakin's artistic interpretation of the Greys' Ghosts (see front cover illustration) is also deserving of much praise, depicting as it does the atmosphere and theme of this volume. John Foreman merits a special mention. His knowledge and unceasing assistance is, like his much loved regiment, second to none.

Information on Lieutenant Thomas Trotter is by courtesy of Mr Alexander Trotter from his family archive. Similarly the information on 'Nelly' is courtesy of the Royal Scots Dragoons Regimental Trust and Major Bruce Ridge.

Thank you also to Diana Birch of Savannah Publications for her excellent support and invaluable, cheerful assistance.

Last and certainly not least, my thanks to Lauren Wakefield BA (Hons) and Ann Mellor for their indefatigable secretarial assistance.

Introduction

The imagination is excited by the thought of large grey horses, ridden by sword wielding, red coated soldiers in black bearskin helmets, galloping menacingly forward in an unstoppable manner. Lady Butler's depiction of the 2nd Dragoons or Royal North British Dragoons (later known as Scots Greys) at Waterloo, leaves an impression few could forget, but just how realistic was this artistic interpretation? Rain sodden uniforms bespattered with mud, sometimes partly obscured by musket holed cloaks, although more realistic, conjures up a less attractive picture.

War is not to be glorified. However, in times of adversity a soldier often displays great qualities – bravery, courage, comradeship – and is willing to make the ultimate sacrifice, his life. With the exception of the hero Sergeant Charles Ewart and high ranking officers such as General William Ponsonby, little is known of the individual men of the Regiment who took part in this charge. Most are lost in history – Greys' Ghosts.

It therefore seemed right to try to determine everything I could about each of these men who fought at Waterloo and thus, in some small way, give them each a true identity and recognition for their sacrifice and courage. With this in mind, this project began and here are the resulting testaments to these hitherto unknown heroes.

Previous works, both Regimental Waterloo Medal Rolls and Rolls of Honour have unwittingly omitted various names, especially of those killed or died of wounds, and so for many years their loss has been unrecorded. I have tried to produce a more accurate roll call of the Scots Greys which would include those killed in action (KIA) and those who died of wounds (DOW), as well as all the remaining survivors. However, it is impossible for me to know for certain if this is a totally accurate list of the men who charged, it can only be an approximation. Those sick, injured, on guard duty, or occasionally a prisoner from earlier skirmishes, may never be known. In all, the names of 458 men are recorded. For any imperfections, I apologise.

I began the project by extracting information from the Waterloo period muster rolls of the 2nd Dragoons during the periods of April-June 1815 and June-September 1815 (WO 12/522). These gave the names of the men likely to have been at Waterloo. The names of those killed during battle were obtained by checking the first muster and confirming their absence from the second. Also the troop to which an individual soldier was assigned was determined. In certain cases, men appeared in different troops, having been transferred to make up the numbers in severely depleted troops. For example, men in Troop 2 on the April muster would appear in Troop 5 in that for September. In certain cases transfers occurred as a result of promotion. Other sources of information included discharge papers WO/97 and WO/120. Late pension claims, WO/116, were also helpful in giving soldiers' details.

Unfortunately, the description book for the Scots Greys could not be located, and so the physical features of some men, for whom there are no discharge papers, were not available. In such cases at least their dates of enlistment are noted. Interestingly, no men were found to be below the height of 5ft 6ins, which suggests a minimum height requirement. Undoubtedly, good horsemanship was a necessary requirement for recruitment into the Greys; a fact on which the ill-fated Cornet, Francis Kinchant, comments in one of his letters written to his parents.

Where possible, places of birth are recorded; these are, as expected, predominately in Scotland. However, there were a significant number of men from England in the Regiment which suggests that recruitment took place from a wide area in Britain. It also underlines the popularity of the Regiment. This fact is further supported by most of the officers being English. Nevertheless, Scotland was proud of its 2nd Dragoons, as were the men proud to serve in it.

Taken from Lady Butler's painting of the charge of the Scots Greys at Waterloo

Waterloo

A detailed account of the battle of Waterloo, 18th June 1815, is beyond the scope of this book. Nevertheless, it is appropriate to mention certain aspects of the engagement which involved the Union Brigade, consisting of the 1st Royals, 2nd Dragoons (Scots Greys), and 6th Dragoons.

The controversial charge of the Union Brigade, and the role of the Scots Greys, is in part clarified by eye-witness accounts found in Siborne's *Waterloo Letters* (1891). However, it should be noted that these accounts were written about 25 years after the event and, as a result, inevitably some details are going to vary. Perhaps, in some way, these different interpretations have added to the intrigue and excitement of the Waterloo campaign.

Some facts, however, are irrefutable. At 1.30pm:

§   D'Erlon's French Infantry was advancing on Wellington's left of centre.
§   The British Infantry (Picton's Division) was in danger of being annihilated.
§   The Union Brigade, commanded by General William Ponsonby, charged down on the French columns.
§   The Royals were attacking Bourgeois' Brigade.
§   The Inniskillings and Scots Greys were attacking the Divisions of Donzelot and Marcognet respectively.

During the battle, Sergeant Ewart, Scots Greys, captured the eagle of the 45th French Infantry Regiment.

In his account, Colonel De Lacey Evans, Aide-de-Camp to General William Ponsonby, confirmed that it was Ponsonby who gave the signal for the Brigade to charge. He also stressed that, after the initial successful charge, General Ponsonby attempted to stop the imprudent and reckless further advance towards the French artillery. However, Ponsonby reluctantly followed his Brigade into the inevitable disaster. This resulted in his death at the hands of French Lancers, the price he paid for not using his better horse which he feared may be injured in the charge.

Lieutenant Charles Wyndham, Scots Greys, who was in Payne's Troop at Waterloo, describes how Major Thomas Hankin, Scots Greys, was injured before the charge and taken to the rear. He refutes the statement that the Scots Greys were in reserve and claims that the Brigade charged in line. His account confirms that he was wounded for the first time a few yards after passing the hedge close to the Highlanders of Pack's Brigade (Picton's Division). Following this, the Greys 'sabred a good many going down the hill'. Some minutes later the second French column was encountered, and Lieutenant Wyndham sustained a second and disabling wound to the foot, which may, ironically, have saved his life.

Colonel J. Muter, 6th Inniskilling Dragoons, confirmed the death of General Ponsonby, which occurred after the charge through the columns of French Infantry. Muter then succeeded to the command of the Brigade until he was wounded near the end of the action. Sir Arthur Clifton (Colonel of the Royals) then took over.

In his recollection of the action, Alex Kennedy Clark, a Captain in the Royals at Waterloo, wrote that the Greys must have charged immediately after the first line as they were 'up and mixed' with the Royals long before they got half way down the slope. The enthusiasm of the Greys can never be doubted. The left of the Brigade (Scots Greys) suffered severely from a body of French Lancers, but Clark does not elaborate on this. The Royals retired, protected by Sir John Vandeleur's Light Cavalry (11th, 12th and 16th Light Dragoons). The 12th Light Dragoons charged down the valley and broke the only French column to remain intact after the disruption by the Union Brigade. They then engaged the French Lancers, who were in pursuit of the remnants of the British Heavy Cavalry. The 16th British Cavalry, led by Vandeleur, also attacked the Lancers, driving them back to the foot of the valley. In achieving this, however, the 12th and 16th Light Cavalry sustained heavy casualties.

The account by Major Robert Winchester of the 92 Highlanders (a Lieutenant at Waterloo) appears to record the events in an accurate and dispassionate manner. The 92nd was ordered by Sir Denis Pack to charge the oncoming French. The Highlanders were about 20 yards from the column when they fired their volley. The French Infantry had just reached the hedge at the side of the road. At this moment, the Scots Greys arrived and doubled around the flanks and centre of the 92nd, where openings were made for them. Both regiments charged together, calling, 'Scotland Forever!'

The Scots Greys actually 'walked' over the column and, in less than three minutes, it was totally destroyed. They then lost control, no longer functioning as a Cavalry regiment, but more like individuals, charging and sabring any enemy they encountered.

Milhaud's French Cavalry Corps and the Lancers attached to D'Erlon's Division were sent into action. Although it was the 6th and 9th Cuirassiers who first engaged the Greys, it was the 7th Cuirassiers who claimed credit for inflicting heavy casualties on them.

It was the 3rd and 4th French Lancers, and not the Polish Lancers, who ruthlessly struck down the vulnerable British Dragoons as they attempted to return to their own lines. It should be noted that there was only one small squadron of Polish Lancers at Waterloo but its lances were equally as sharp as many men in the Scots Greys found to their cost!

The loss of the Union Brigade was certainly noticed by Wellington's Army later in the battle, especially as they were not able successfully to pursue the French retreat.

Despite this, the Union Brigade's achievements were many, including:

§   The support and rescue of Wellington's left of centre and, by so doing, saving Picton's Division from possible annihilation.

§   The capture of more than 2000 French prisoners.

§   The destruction of 15 French guns.

§   The capture of the Eagle of the French 45th Infantry.

§   The demonstration of French vulnerability.

The Waterloo Medal 1815

Instituted in 1816, this was the first campaign medal to be issued to all ranks. It was much prized by the victorious soldiers of Wellington's army. However, for the brave men who fought in several campaigns in the Peninsular War, it only served to aggravate the painful lack of recognition of their earlier magnificent achievements. Therefore, the medal was greeted initially with mixed feelings. It would not be until 1848, when the Military General Service Medal 1793–1814 was instituted to recognise earlier campaigns, that justice was done, but by this time many men had died unrewarded. Despite this, the Waterloo Medal was regarded as a badge or mark of success and most recipients wore it with pride. Some enjoyed the benefits of free ale in exchange for stories about famous encounters with the French, well exemplified by Dickson (page 91) and his account of the battle.

This silver medal measures 3.5cms in diameter. The obverse shows the head of the Prince Regent wearing a laurel wreath. On the reverse is the seated figure of Victory, holding a palm branch in her right hand and an olive branch in her left. Below the seated figure are the word 'WATERLOO' and the date 'JUNE 18. 1815', while above is the name of 'WELLINGTON'. The naming, on the rim, is in large impressed Roman capitals. Although the medal was originally issued with a steel clip suspender, it is not uncommon for this to have been replaced by a suspender of the recipient's choice.

The naming on medals awarded to the Scots Greys shows the individual soldier's name in Roman capitals, followed by 2nd or R N BRITT. REG. DRAG (Royal North British Regiment of Dragoons the former name of the Scots Greys). Spaces are filled with asterisks. Occasionally, a medal can be seen named to a soldier in the 2nd DRAGOONS. This may be a later issue, probably because the man was killed in action. It should be noted that awards of the medal were not automatically made to those killed in action, though some awards were issued later on application from the deceased's family. Collectors need to be aware of fake medals and expert opinion may be required to confirm authenticity.

At least two medals are known to exist to officers of the Scots Greys who were killed in action. They are those to Lieutenant Colonel James Inglis Hamilton (National Museum of Scotland) and Cornet Francis Kinchant (private collection). The latter is named in the later style. The style of naming on the former is not known.

Sometimes soldiers had difficulty in receiving their medals. This occurred for a variety of reasons which included: discharge from the army, chronic illness or wounds, or transfer to a different regiment. National Archives document WO 100/12, the Return of the Non-Effective Waterloo Men, reveals that the medals to officers and men, such as Captain Edward Payne, Sergeant Richard Hayward, Sergeant Charles Ewart and Private Andrew M'Kendrick, were returned to Canterbury in April 1816. All of these medals eventually got to the rightful recipients and still exist today in private collections or, in the case of Ewart, in the National Museum of Scotland. Sadly, this was not the case for Privates Robert Hair, Henry Eaves, James Button and David Henderson, who never received their medals because they died before this was possible.

The Scots Greys Museum is in possession of twelve Waterloo Medals (see pages 14-16, List of Extant Medals). (In the interest of correctness, I should point out that the Scots Greys Museum is now part of the Regimental Museum of the Royal Scots Dragoon Guards in Edinburgh).

Medals Known To Be Extant

Officers	Provenance
Lieutenant Colonel James Ingles Hamilton	National War Museum Scotland
Major Isaac Blake Clarke[3]	Sold from the family to USA
Captain Thomas Charles Fenton	Regimental Museum
Captain Edward Payne	Glendining September 1993
Lieutenant George Home Falconer	Ambrose Elson collection 1963
Lieutenant James Gape	Unknown
Lieutenant James Reginald Torin Graham	Border Regiment Museum
Lieutenant Archibald James Hamilton[1]	J B Hayward & Son
Adjutant Lieutenant Henry MacMillan	Dr John Cruickshank collection
Lieutenant John Mills	Regimental Museum
Lieutenant Francis Stupart	Regimental Museum
Lieutenant Charles Wyndham[2]	J B Hayward & Son
Cornet Francis Charlton Kinchant	Robert Gottlieb collection
Surgeon Robert Daun	Regimental Museum
Saddler Sergeant Alexander Wallace	Oakley collection 1953
Troop Sergeant Major William Perrie	London Stamp Exchange 1985
Troop Sergeant Major James Russell	Buckland Dix & Wood 1994
Paymaster Sergeant William Bayne	Dix Noonan Webb 2002
Sergeant William Clarke	Glendining 1903
Sergeant William Dickie	Robert Gottlieb collection
Sergeant David Dunn	Buckland Dix & Wood
Sergeant Charles Ewart	National War Museum Scotland
Sergeant John Gillies	Glendining November 1981
Sergeant William Harvey	Glendining 1926
Sergeant Richard Hayward	Richard Kirch 1992
Sergeant John McNeil	Matthew Taylor collection
Sergeant William Porteous	Buckland Dix & Wood
Sergeant Thomas Soars	Regimental Museum
Sergeant William Swan	Author's collection
Sergeant John Tannock	Christie 1965
Corporal John Craig	Jim Bullock Militaria 2008
Corporal John Dickson	National War Museum Scotland
Corporal Alexander Gardiner	Dix Noonan Webb 2005
Corporal John Long	Glendining 1990
Corporal Michael Nelson	Regimental Museum
Corporal Samuel Tar	Buckland Dix & Wood 1994
Corporal Robert Thompson	Dix Noonan Webb 2010
Corporal Alexander Wilson	Sotheby 1995
Trumpeter Thomas Allen	Sotheby 1880

Trumpeter Peter Buncle	Spink 2005
Trumpeter John Henry Sibold	Buckland Dix & Wood 1994
Paymaster William Dawson	Dix Noonan Webb 2005
Private John Alexander	Allison collection
Private David Anderson	Glendining 1956
Private John Atherley	Glendining 1922
Private John Ballantyne	Private collection
Private William Ballantyne	Unknown
Private Samuel Boulter	Glendining 1977
Private Cunningham Bowes	Unknown
Private Joseph Brazier	Glendining 1903
Private Stephen Brookes	Christie 1965 (ex-Mackenzie collection)
Private Francis Brown	Glendining 1964
Private James Bruce	Liverpool Medal Co 1984
Private James Bullock	Glendining 1987
Private George Butler	Dix Noonan Webb 2004
Private John Clarke	Bonham 2007
Private John Collier	Glendining 1970
Private Adam Colquhoun	Regimental Museum
Private David Craig	Spink 1949
Private David Crighton	Sotheby 1986
Private John Crombie	Unknown
Private William Cunningham	Glendining 1977, Allison collection
Private Robert Currie	Spink 2003
Private John Dunn	Lockdales 2009
Private Thomas Fergus	Baldwin 1975
Private James Frame	Glendining 1939 (E E Needes collection)
Private Thomas Goods	Sotheby 1928 (Colonel Murray collection)
Private Alexander Gourley	Glendining 1989
Private Robert Gourley	Spink 1979
Private George Gray	E E Needes collection 1925
Private William Gunn	Glendining 1935
Private William Hickling	Glendining 1943 (Gaskell collection)
Private David Kelly	Glendining 1919
Private James Kennedy	Dix Noonan Webb
Private John Lane (Land)	Christie 1965
Private William Levitt	Allison collection
Private John Liddle	Regimental Museum
Private William Lockead (Lochead)	Glendining 1992 (Jubilee collection)
Private John McKechney	Liverpool Medal Co 1984
Private Andrew M'Kendrick	Glendining May 1957 (ex-Ernie Bell collection)
Private William M'Kinley	Dix Noonan Webb
Private Hugh M'Lelland	Spink 1997
Private John Martin	Dix Noonan Webb 2004
Private David Mathie	Bostock Militaria 2006
Private Andrew Muir	Unknown

Private Thomas Oman	Spink 1878
Private Edward Noaks (Noakes)	Ian Laidler Medals 1998
Private Henry Palmer	Dowell of Edinburgh 1926
Private James Paterson	Glendining 1990
Private Robert Paterson	Unknown
Private William Pearson	Regimental Museum
Private William Provan	Christie 1990
Private David Rampton	Glendining 1903
Private Thomas Robertson	Regimental Museum
Private Samuel Sifton	Dix Noonan Webb 2010
Private Robert Smellie	Dix Noonan Webb 1993
Private William Storrie	Regimental Museum
Private Peter Swan	Author's collection
Private William Sykes	Regimental Museum
Private Jonathan Taylor	Dix Noonan Webb 2005
Private Robert Temple	Hyde Greg collection 1887
Private Joseph Tucky	Dix Noonan Webb 2005
Private John Watson	Unknown
Private William Watt	Spink 1997
Private Thomas Wilmot	Glendining 1990
Private Alexander Young	Sotheby 1995
Private Nathaniel Young	Sotheby 1978

Where possible the provenance is taken from the most recent reputable source or auction house catalogue. In some cases, medals may not have been seen or even been in circulation for many years.

1. The medals to Lieutenant Colonel Hamilton, Sergeant Ewart and Corporal Dickson are in the National War Museum Scotland.
2. Medals in pairs or groups are rare. Although several officers served in the Peninsular War, there is only one who received the Military General Service Medal 1793-1814 in addition to the Waterloo Medal; this was Lieutenant Charles Wyndham. Corporal Dickson was awarded the Long Service & Good Conduct Medal and can be seen wearing the pair in his portrait page 93). In addition, Corporal David McGowan, Private George Willet, and Private John Thompson received Long Service and Good Conduct Medals.
3. Sometimes high ranking officers were rewarded with decorations. Major Isaac Clarke and Captain Cheney both received the Companion of the Bath (CB). The former also received the Russian Order of St Anne. Major Hankin received a Knighthood.

Scots Greys
Waterloo Medal Roll

12 Second or Royal N. Brit. Dragoons

#	Field & Staff Officers			Privates		#
				Privates	Jas. Gibson	37
1	Major	Isaac B. Clarke			H.Y. Head	38
2		T. P. Hankin			John Hervie	39
3	Adjutant	H.Y. Macmillan			Jos. Jarvie	40
4	Surgeon	Robt. Daun			David Kally	41
5	A. Surgr.	Jas. Alexander			Wm. Kidd	42
6	Vt. Surgn.	John Fugg			Jas. Knox	43
7	Regt. Dr. Mr.	John Lennox			John Livingston	44
8	Pay Mr.	Wm. Dawson			Wm. Luke	45
					Adam Mc. Cue	46
	Capt. late Barnards Troop				Jas. Mc. Millan	47
					John Marshall	48
9	Lieutenant	G. K. Falconer			David Mathie	49
10	Troop Sery. Mr.	Wm. Perrie			Robt. Mathews	50
11	Reg. Sery. Maj.	Wm. Crawford			Jas. Nairn	51
12	Pay Mast. Sry.	Wm. Bayne			Thos. Nicols	52
13	Armr. as Sry.	Jas. Bray			Wm. Pakush	53
14	Saddler as Sery.	Alext. Wallace			David Portland	54
15	Serjeants	John Gillier			Wm. Rowan	55
16		Wm. Porteous			Wm. Robertson	56
17		Jno. White			Job Rood	57
18	Corps.	Alexr. Hall			Jas. Rowan	58
19		Alexr. Sikh			Wm. Taylor	59
20		John Scott			Jno. Watson	60
21		Hugh Rylae			Robert Wall	61
22	Trumpeter	Hump. Steverson			Wm. Wells	62
23	Privates	John Aitkin			Wm. Williamson	63
24		John Andrew			David Wilson	64
25		Jas. Ballantyne			John White	65
26		Edwd. Bell			Thos. Young	66
27		Isaac Bell				
28		John Blain		Captain Payne's Troop		
29		Wm. Bromley				
30		Jas. Bullock		Captain	Edwd. Payne	67
31		John Callendar		Lieutenants	Arch. Hamilton	68
32		John Chambling			Chas. Wyndham	69
33		Jas. Clachan		Troop Sry. Mr.	Wm. Robertson	70
34		Jas. Drummond		Serjeants	Jas. Bullock	71
35		Geo. Fiddes			David Dunn	72
36		Jas. Frame			John Mc. Neil	73

2nd Regt or Royal N. Britt: Dragoons

No.	Rank	Name	Rank	Name	No.
74	Serjeants	Wm Somerville	Privates	Jas Masterton	114
75	Corporals	Geo. Edwards		Geo. Mauchlin	15
76		Geo. Milward		Wm Merrie	16
77		Michl Nelson		Robt Miller	17
78	Privates	David Anderson		Jas Patterson	18
79		Alexr Armour		Robt Patterson	19
80		John Bishop		Hugh Pattison	120
81		Alexr Borland		Andrew Peden	21
82		Jos. Brazier		Saml Sifton	22
83		John Brown		Jas Smith	23
84		Thos Bullock		Wm Smith	24
85		Alexr Campbell		Jas Struthers	25
86		Colin Campbell		Jos. Tuchy	26
87		Robt Carnaby		Jas Waile	27
88		Wm Clarke		Jas Walker	28
89		Wm Cunningham		Fras Wells	29
90		David Dick		Geo. Willet	130
91		Henry Eaves		Wm Wilkerson	31
92		Peter Evans		Wm Wilson	32
93		Thos Fergus		Robt Wilson	33
94		Wm Fleming		Archd Wright	34
95		Peter Gibson			
96		Alexr Gourley	Captain Cheney's Troop.		
97		John Hamilton			
98		Jas Hart	Captain	Edwd Cheney	135
99		Wm Hickling	Lieutenants	Fras Stupart	36
100		Wm Hill		Jas Gape	37
1		Alexr Hunter	Troop Serjt Major	Alexr Dingwall	38
2		Alexr Ingram			
3		Jas Lipsley	Serjeants	Donald Campbell	39
4		Richd Lee		Wm Dickie	140
5		Wm Levitt		Wm Harvey	41
6		Geo. Longworth		Alexr Rennie	42
7		John McKechny	Corporals	Robt Hair	43
8		David McLelland		Wm Laird	44
9		Hugh McLelland		John Long	45
110		Alexr McLeod		Jas Rofs	46
11		Jas McLintoch	Trumpeter	Jas H. Sibold	47
12		Wm Mackie	Privates	Geo. Allison	48
13		John Martin		Matthew Anderson	49

2nd Reg.t or Royal N. Britt: Dragoons

150	Privates	Arch.d Bell		Rob.t Stirling	190
51		Hugh Beckett		W.m Sterling	91
52		John Bush		Tho.s Stott	92
53		Cha.s Burges		Tho.s Temperley	93
54		Ja.s Button		Rob.t Temple	94
55		Jno Calder		Ja.s Thompson	95
56		Sam.l Clarke		Jno Toman	96
57		Arch.d Craig		John Wallace	97
58		David Cughton		W.m Watt	98
59		Tho.s Crowe			
160		John Crombie	Capt.r Poole's Troop		
61		Major Dickinson			
62		Peter Drysdale	Capt.r	Ja.s Poole	199
63		John Fraser	Lieut.t	Ja.s Wemyss	200
64		Geo. Gray	Troop S.ey.t	Ja.s Russell	1
65		W.m Gunn	Serjeants	Jno Bishop	2
66		Ja.s Hamilton S.r		Arch.d Johnston	3
67		Ja.s Hamilton J.r		Tho.s Stoddart	4
68		David Henderson	Corporals	Alex.r Gardner	5
69		Adam Hepburn		Ja.s Nelson	6
170		W.m Hubbard		Jno Wallace	7
71		Tho.s Johnston	Trumpeter	Peter Buncle	8
72		John Judd	Privates	John Alexander	9
73		W.m Lockead		Ja.s Bruce	210
74		Andrew M.c Clure		Ja.s Crawford	11
75		Archibald M.c Farlan		David Craig	12
76		John M.c Intire		Joseph Crowe	13
77		And.w M.c Kendrick		Alex.r Donaldson	14
78		W.m M.c Kinley		W.m Erskine	15
79		Alex.r M.c Pherson		Gavin Gibson	16
80		Rob.t Makin		John Gibson	17
81		Ja.s Mann		Rob.t Gilchrist	18
82		W.m Mathie		Tho.s Goods	19
83		Tho.s Oman		Ja.s Kenneday	220
84		David Rampton		Alex.r Lauder	21
85		Ja.s Renalds		Andrew Lees	22
86		Andrew Scott		W.m Locks	23
87		Ja.s Scott		Rob.t Lawrie	24
88		John Spraike		David M.c Goun	25
89		John Stirling		Fred.k M.c Vicar	26

2nd Reg.t or Royal N: Britt Dragoons

No.	Rank	Name		Rank	Name	No.
No. 227	Privates	John Miller		Privates	James Brown	264
28		Andrew Muir			John Brobin	65
29		John Nelson			Geo: Butler	66
230		Edwd Noaks			Adam Colquhoun	67
31		Henry Palmer			John Coltur	68
32		Thos Philips			Robt Craig	69
33		James Ratcliff			John Dalguil	270
34		Jas Richardson			Wm Dunlop	71
35		Thos Robertson			Jno Dunn	72
36		Wm Robertson			John Gillies	73
37		John Rowatt			Wm Gordon	74
38		John Salmon			Robt Growley	75
39		Mattw Scott			Robt Greig	76
240		Robt Smellie			John Harkness	77
41		Robt Stevenson			John Henderson	78
42		Adam Tait			Henry Hodkinson	79
43		John Thompson			Wm Jones	280
44		James Tovie			Saml Kennair	81
45		John Work			James King	82
46		Andw White			John Lane	83
47		Robt Wilson			David McMl	84
48		Wm Willis			John McGee	85
49		Wm Wright			Wm Mackie	86
250		Alexr Young			Wm McNair	87
51		Nathl Young			John Mathews	88
					James Montgomery	89
	Captain Vernor's Troop				John Moore	290
52	Captain	Robt Vernor			Wm Patton Sr	91
53	Lieutt	John Mills			Wm Patton Jr	92
54	Troop Serjt Major	Wm McMullen			Wm Park	93
55	Serjeants	Wm Clarke			Robt Reid	94
56		Chas Ewart			Thos Reid	95
57		John Tannoch			Wm Ross	96
58	Corporals	John Dickson			Jas Smith	97
59		Saml Tar			Wm Smith	98
260		Alexr Wilson			Wm Sykes	99
61	Trumpeter	Jos: Reeves			Ebenr Thompson	300
62	Privates	John Atherley			John Veazy	1
63		Fredk Brown			Robt Wallace	2
					Thos Watson	3

2nd Reg.t or Royal N. Britt. Dragoons.

No.	Rank	Name	Rank	Name	No.
304	Privates	Rich.d Wharan	Privates	Arch.d Kean	341
5		John Wise		Ja.s Kean	42
				Sam.l Keeble	43
	Capt.n Fenton's Troop			Sam.l Kinder	44
				John Liddle	45
6	Captain	Tho.s C. Fenton		Rob.t Littlejohn	46
7	Lieutenant	J. R. T. Graham		Jos. Macre	47
8	Serjeants	James Andrew		Peter Miller	48
9		R.d Hayward		John Mitchell	49
310		Tho.s Soars		W.m Pearson	350
11		W.m Swan		W.m Reid	51
12	Corporals	John Craig		John Ross	52
13		Tho.s Davis		W.m Smith	53
14		Rob.t Thompson		Peter Swan	54
15		John Allan		Jon: Taylor	55
16	Trumpeter	Henry Boing		And.w Thompson	56
17	Privates	Tho.s Anderson		John Watson	57
18		John Arklie		Tho.s Wilmot	58
19		Jas. Armour	Supplementary		
20		W.m Ballantyne	Capt.n Vernor's Troop —		
21		Geo. Biddolph	Privates	W.m Storrie	59
22		Alex.r Blackadder		Jas. Liddle	360
23		Benj.t Boulter	From a List from J. P. Hankin		
24		Cunningham Bowg	L.t Coll.		
25		Step. Brooks	25 th April 1816		
26		Adam Brown			
27		John Campbell			
28		John Clarke			
29		Rob.t Currie			
330		W.m Dick			
31		John Dobbie			
32		John Ferguson			
33		John Gould			
34		Jas. Green			
35		W.m Howie			
36		Alex.r Hunter			
37		Hugh Hunter			
38		Rob.t Hunter			
39		Arch.d Hatton			
340		Jas. Jones			

The Waterloo Medal, reverse,
to Trooper David Craig (Pooles Troop)

Scots Greys
Waterloo Roll of Honour

The official casualties of the Scots Greys were: 105 men were killed or died of wounds; 93 were wounded (see, 'Les Terribles Chevaux Gris', Major R.B. Anderson, in the journal of the Scots Greys). The names that appear on the Roll of Honour below were either killed in action (KIA) or died of wounds (DOW). Those categorised as DOW include men who died years later from their wounds. The most meaningful definition of this term would be that it covers men who died as a direct result of injury sustained in battle, or from a battle injury which led to death in the longer term. It includes chronic illness from long-standing sepsis, or debility from malnutrition arising from fistulae.

Men missing from Almack's Roll

Almack's Roll of Honour, which appeared in the Regimental history (1908), omits 17 names which have since been identified as fatal casualties. These names appear with an asterisk (*) and in bold type on the Roll of Honour that follows. Until now, the sacrifice of these men has been unrecognised, and on this basis they may aptly, and more than most, be called Greys' Ghosts.

The rest of the Roll is based on that produced by Almack, though with corrections. It is a tribute to those in the 2nd Dragoons, who lost their lives fighting at Waterloo.

ROLL OF HONOUR

Name and Rank	Place of Birth
Officers	
Colonel Hamilton, James Inglis	Tayantroga, America
Captain Barnard, Charles Levyns	Cave Castle, Yorkshire
Captain Reignolds, Thomas	
Lieutenant Carruthers, James	Annandale, Dumfriesshire
Lieutenant Trotter, Thomas	Morton Hall, Midlothian
Cornet Kinchant, Francis C.	Easton, Herefordshire
Cornet Shuldham, Lemuel	Marlesford, Suffolk
Cornet Westby, Edward	Thornhill, Dublin
Non-Commissioned Officers	
Troop Sergeant Major Weir, John	Mauchline
Sergeant Pollock, Arthur	Blantyre
Sergeant Rennie, George	Whitburn
Sergeant Strudwick, James	Ryegate (Reigate)

Corporals and Privates

Private Aldcorn, William	Stichill
Private Arthur, John	Cumbernauld
Private Black, Alexander	Dunfermline
Private Brinsby (Brimsly), William	Horton
Private Brookes, John	Heaton Norris [Stockport]
Private Brown, Samuel	Nuttsford [Knutsford]
Private Brown, Thomas	Alnwick
Private Bryce, James*	
Private Bryce, William	Bo'ness
Private Butler, George	Castleton
Private Christie, William	Auchterarder
Private Coupland, John	Kirkmahoe
Corporal Craig, John	Barony
Private Craig, Robert	Rutherglen
Private Craig, William	Paisley
Private Dawson, Joshua	Otley
Private Dawson, Thomas	Ambleside
Private Dodds, John	Berwick on Tweed
Private Donaldson, Robert	Barony
Private Dougal, John	Barony
Private Eaves, Henry*	
Private Ellingworth, George	Brotherton
Private Ferguson, James	Barony
Private Forbes, Duncan	Irverie
Private Frost, John	Tutbury
Private Grey, Alexander	Paisley
Private Hall, John	Cambletown
Private Hamilton, Robert*	**Kilmarnock**
Corporal Harper, James*	**Kilmarnock**
Private Harris, Thomas*	**Broughton**
Private Harvie, Allan*	**Hayfield**
Trumpeter Hutchinson, Hugh*	**Galston**
Private Jamison, John	Barony
Private Johnston, Gavin	Old Monkland
Private Kenmuir, Samuel*	**Kilmarnock**
Private Kerr, Alexander	Ayr
Private Kidd, John	Kinross
Private Kitchen, George*	**Broughton**
Private Knight, Andrew	Inveresk
Private Law, Samuel*	
Private Leach, William	Northwich
Private Love, James	Dalsey (?)
Private Lyle, Robert	Killochan
Private Lyon, James*	
Private MacKay, Alexander	Glasgow

Private MacKie, Robert	Blantyre
Private McAll, David*	**Fauls**
Private McAlla, George	Carnwath
Private McArthur, John	Barony
Private McAuley, Hugh	Paisley
Private McCulloch, John	Kilmarnock
Private McFarlan, Andrew	Glasgow
Private McFarlan, James*	
Private McIndoe, Robert*	**Govan**
Private McKechney, Daniel	Greenock
Private McLauchlan, James	Sanquhar
Private McLauchlan, John	Dumfries
Private McPherson, Angus	Moidart
Private Mather, Gavin	Hamilton
Private Merrie, Hugh	
Private Millar, John	Old Monkland
Private Millar, William	Egham
Private Mitchell, William	Kilmarnock
Private Muirhead, Robert	Glasgow
Private Murdoch, William	Auchinleck
Private Murray, Peter	Tippermuir
Private Picken, David	Stewarton
Private Priestley, Luke	Portsham
Private Pye, James*	**Astley**
Private Rayburn, John	Paisley
Private Robertson, John	Paisley
Private Robertson, Thomas	Neilston
Private Rolland, David	Strathblane
Private Rose, James	Glasgow
Private Rowatt, William*	**Kirkintilloch**
Private Sawers, John	Rutherglen
Corporal Scott, John	Muiravonside
Private Senior, John	Emley
Private Simmons, John	Bunbury (Burnbury)
Private Smith, James	Kilmarnock
Private Stoddart, David	Newbattle
Private Sutherland, William	Cambuslang
Private Taylor, Robert	Barony
Private Taylor, Thomas	Fordingbridge
Private Tennant, Robert*	**Dewny**
Private Turner, George	Yetholm
Private Turner, John	Alnwick
Private Urie, John	Gorbals
Private Walker, Alexander	Tengle
Private Whitton, John	Packington
Private Wotherspoon, Peter	Abernethy

Private Wylie, Andrew   Stewarton
Private Young, Robert   Paisley

Mortality Rate

It is interesting to note the differences in the mortality rate (MR) between the troops. The MR is calculated using the following formula:

§   MR   =   mortality rate, expressed as a percentage:

$$MR = \frac{KIA + DOW}{NT\ (number\ of\ men\ in\ troop)} \times 100$$

These were:

Barnard's Troop	24.3%
Payne's Troop	8.2%
Cheney's Troop	13.3%
Poole's Troop	28.6%
Vernor's Troop	29.7%
Fenton's Troop	23.0%

These figures are approximate as the exact number of chargers will never be known. There is also some doubt as to the troops in which Lieutenant Carruthers and Trotter, and Cornets Shuldham and Westby charged.

The relatively high mortality could be simply explained by the ferocity of the fighting. However, other factors must include the over enthusiasm and imprudence of the troopers, the exhausted horses, and the ruthlessness and skill of the French Lancers. Also, it should be emphasised that the deaths of the Brigade Commander General William Ponsonby, Lieutenant Colonel James Inglis Hamilton and his ADC Major Thomas Reignolds and the injury to Major Thomas Hankin must have contributed in part to indiscipline and the subsequent high casualties.

Perhaps the lack of experience in combat as well as seniority contributed to the imprudent, over zealous charge made on the French Artillery. The list illustrates the relatively recent the dates of many officers' commissions.

Captain Charles Levyns Barnard	February 1815
Captain Thomas Charles Fenton	February 1815
Captain Edward Payne	February 1815
Lieutenant James Carruthers	February 1815
Lieutenant Archibald James Hamilton	February 1815
Lieutenant Thomas Trotter	March 1815
Lieutenant James Gape	May 1815
Lieutenant James R. T. Graham	May 1815
Lieutenant Charles Wyndham	May 1815
Cornet Francis C. Kinchant	January 1815
Cornet Lemuel Shuldham	January 1815

Five of these officers were killed and three were wounded.

However, such data and statistics need to be balanced against the fact that Barnard, Hamilton, Fenton and Wyndham all had combat experience in the Peninsular War. Nevertheless, the evidence of the Regiment's lack of seniority cannot, and should not, be dismissed. It is not sufficient to say, as has been argued, that they continued to charge because 'they wanted to'. In spite of this, the courage and heroism displayed by the Greys is beyond question. The challenge and defiance of the Union Brigade, in the face of the masses of the seemingly invincible French Army, was a lesson and great encouragement to the rest of the British Army and its allies – a lesson which contributed to Wellington's eventual victory.

Wounded

Service personnel classified as wounded are those known to have received an injury, directly or indirectly, during engagement with the enemy. There are three kinds of wounds documented on a soldier's record (WO97 series at the National Archives): non-specific; specific; coincidental.

Non-specific wounds are usually recorded simply as wound(s) received at Waterloo. The site and cause of the wound are not stated. The severity of the wound may be stated or only revealed if the soldier's condition deteriorates and he then dies. An example is that of Private James Armour, whose record states: 'Received Wounds at Waterloo'.

In the case of specific wounds, the site and cause(s) are stated. A good example is found on Corporal Samuel Tar's record which states that at Waterloo he was severely wounded by a bayonet in the left foot, by a lance in the left leg, and between the shoulders.

To have suffered from lance wounds suggests that they were sustained towards the end of the Scots Greys charge when they encountered the French Lancers. This is supported by Corporal John Dickson's account of the battle. Another example is that of David Crighton whose record states that he sustained a gunshot wound to the belly. This was probably thought to be fatal but it was not so, hence his inclusion on Almack's Roll of Honour was incorrect.

A coincidental injury was one not suffered directly at the hands of the enemy, but one which rendered an individual unfit for action or further service in the army. The most obvious example is Major Hankin who was thrown from his horse before the charge. Fortunately he recovered from these injuries and later gained promotion and a knighthood. Also Private William Provan is described as having an ulcerated leg from a contusion sustained at Waterloo.

The effects of wounds and injuries sustained at Waterloo are in many ways difficult to imagine, as there were no intravenous fluids or blood for resuscitation, no antibiotics to combat infection, and no general anaesthesia to facilitate major surgery. It is amazing how so many soldiers survived their traumas, a credit to their strength and resilience, as well as good surgery.

Wyndham (Siborne, 1891) describes how one man named Loch (Lock(s)) sustained 18 lance wounds and survived. In his excellent book *Men of Steel* (2007), Crumplin gives a good insight into the nature and treatment of wounds in Napoleonic warfare.

Charles Ewart

Sergeant Charles Ewart was a reluctant hero, just a soldier doing his duty. His exceptional horsemanship, dexterity with a sword, and strong physique enabled him to achieve the magnificent feat of capturing a French Eagle. The capture of the Eagle of the 45th French Infantry Regiment has become part of Waterloo history and enhanced the reputation of the Scots Greys. The Eagle has now been incorporated into the Regiment's badge.

What of the man who performed this act of heroism? The attempts to portray Charles Ewart as a national hero were immediately successful. However, it would seem that he may not have been too comfortable in this role. For example, when asked to make a speech at a dinner in his honour, he replied that he would prefer to face the French again rather than deliver a speech. This reflects the modest and perhaps laconic nature of this man which he demonstrated on more than one occasion throughout his life.

The caring and sensitive nature of Ewart was displayed some time before his Waterloo exploits. In 1794, when the Greys were passing through Holland, they had to march during the night. It was thought that the sound of a baby crying could be heard in the darkness. Although the sound was first dismissed as not worthy of a second thought, Ewart insisted on investigating despite his sceptical comrades. Soon a baby was found in the arms of his mother. The baby was well wrapped but not so the mother who had died from hypothermia. Ewart extricated the baby from the lifeless limbs and wrapped him in his own thick warm blanket. The baby was taken to the next village where Ewart sought assistance from a Dutch woman who was suckling a child of her own. She was so moved by the tragic story and promised to take care of the child until other members of his family could be found. Fourteen years later, Ewart learnt that the child had survived and had become a healthy young man.

After retirement from the army, he did not return to his native Scotland. There is little doubt that had he returned, he would have been showered with gifts and praise. Perhaps the truth was that he was happy with his wife, Maggie, in England, away from the spotlight and without the need to live up to the reputation lavished upon him after his triumph in Flanders.

Ensign Ewart retired from the army, 5th Veteran Battalion, in 1821. He lived in Tranmere and then in Ulverston. His next place of residence was Hampson Street, Salford, where he took up employment teaching the skills of swordsmanship. Amongst his friends there were Mr R P Livingstone, later to become Mayor, and Deputy Constable Diggles. Unfortunately his stay in Salford was marred by the theft of a silver cup presented by his comrades in the Scots Greys. The culprit was apprehended but not before the cup was melted down for its precious metal. The thief was punished by deportation.

About 1830, Ewart and his wife Maggie went to live in the more rural Davyhulme, now part of Trafford, Manchester, where they lived in a cottage on Bents Lane, opposite Davyhulme Hall. It is said that the former Waterloo veteran was employed at the hall, and was probably responsible for its security.

Amongst his friends and admirers was a young boy, Andrew Taylor, of whom Charles Ewart was particularly fond. On occasions, the boy would be treated to an account of the brave soldier's exploits. When the heroic sergeant died in 1846, he left to his young friend a framed portrait of himself, the

Bowman's watercolour of Charles Ewart

leather razor case he carried in his haversack at Waterloo and a copy of a newspaper telling of the Eagle's capture. The small boy's hero-worship lasted all of his life and this affection and admiration for Ewart was passed down to his daughter, Jane. The portrait of Ewart hung on her cottage wall in Davyhulme.

The portrait is of immense interest because it is unique. The painting is a watercolour by a local artist, Richard Bowman, who was a neighbour and friend of Charles Ewart., which probably explains why he came to do the painting. It is thought that it was completed two years before Ewart's death when he was 75 years old. The painting was eventually acquired by George B. Blair and bequeathed to Manchester City Art Galleries in 1941, where it is now in storage.

The whereabouts of Ewart's Waterloo Medal was not known until it appeared in the Gaskell sale 1908 and was purchased by the prolific collector E.E. Needes. It remained in that collection until it was sold following his death in 1939. The final purchaser was the Scottish United Services Museum, which paid what was at the time the princely sum of £65.

Although it is a cliché to say that behind every successful man is a good woman, it seems to have been true in Charles Ewart's case. Maggie Ewart has been described as an energetic, diminutive figure, whose head barely reached her husband's chest. She certainly was not lacking in spirit and courage, amply demonstrated when she followed her husband to Waterloo. After the battle she sought his whereabouts, not knowing he had been ordered back to Brussels by General Ponsonby. Her search to locate what she believed to be his dead body was in vain. Eventually she rested at a nearby blacksmith where she was eventually reunited with her beloved hero, whom she greeted with a strong embrace.

Not much else is known about the couple, their relationship and their lives, however a little further investigation has revealed a few details. A search of the Muster Rolls (WO 12/510-522) between April 1810 and August 1812, shows that Ewart was stationed in Manchester and at Blackburn Barracks. This is almost certainly when he met Maggie. It is interesting to note that he was reduced to Private on 9th February 1812, most likely the result of a 'Bacchanalian indiscretion'. However, he was soon restored to Corporal on 25th September 1813. Perhaps the influence of his new wife was beneficial?

Reference to a 1828 Circular to officers, when Ewart was already retired from the 5th Veteran Battalion, confirms that he got married on 31st January 1812 at St. Mary's Church, Manchester.

Charles Ewart died on 23rd March 1846, aged 77 years, in Davyhulme. Maggie Ewart died ten years later on 26th August 1856, aged 72 years . They are buried in separate graves. Maggie is in the Geddes family grave, St Michael's Church , Flixton, Manchester, while the brave sergeant now rests in his native Scotland, on the esplanade of Edinburgh Castle .

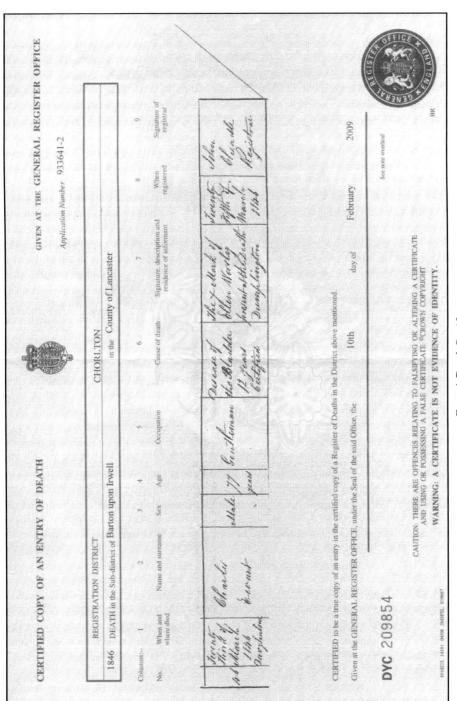

Ewart's Death Certificate

The Fa'kirk Dizzen
(or Falkirk 13)

During the course of this study of the men of the 2nd Dragoons (also known as the Scots Greys) at Waterloo, it was found that 13 men of the Regiment came from Falkirk. Seemingly, all took part in the famous charge of the Union Brigade (1st, 2nd and 6th Dragoons). These men were known colloquially as the 'Fa'kirk Dizzen' (Love, 1945).

The Scots Greys were the premier Cavalry regiment in Scotland and, arguably, the best in Britain. Six troops, about 420 men in total, were sent to Belgium in June 1815, to assist in the fight against Napoleon's army which was threatening to overrun Europe. The charge of the Union Brigade played an important part in the success of the British Army at Waterloo. The Heavy Cavalry rode through the menacing French Infantry, cutting them down with sabres. The French 45th Regiment was almost decimated by the ferocity of the charge. The Scots Greys later lost control and continued to charge the oncoming French until they met the French Cavalry and Lancers who exacted severe revenge. The Greys sustained 50 per cent casualties – a high price for their initial success.

Love retells the traditional story that on that day, 18th June 1815, several of the 13 from Falkirk were lying in a group before their Regiment formed; as legions of horse and foot began to pour into the field, one of the 'Bairns' said to his comrades, "Of what does this put you in mine?" "Jist o' the last Tryst o' Fa'kirk," answered another.

James Love was able to name two of the men as James Masterton and Thomas Nicol, because they went on to live the longest. The remaining 11 appear to have been Peter Miller, Alexander M'Pherson, John Wise (also recorded as Wyse), Ebenezer Thompson, John Callender, John Livingston, Archibald Hutton, William Mackie, Corporal John Scott and two of Nicol's cousins – probably Robert and John Miller.

Naming the two cousins is more problematic. No other Nicol(s) appears on the Waterloo Muster. Roll. If Tam's mother did not have any sisters, then we might be looking for two more men with the surname 'Miller'. There are two such on the Muster – Robert and John.

So far we have 12 men and are looking for 13 – a baker's dozen (of whom at least three were in fact bakers!). The chief candidate for the remaining place is Corporal John Scott, a labourer, from Muiravonside. He was in Payne's Troop and was killed at Waterloo. Whilst not strictly from the town or parish of Falkirk, it would have been his usual market town.

It is strange that a small provincial town such as Falkirk should provide so many men for this elite Cavalry regiment. There is little in the trades of the men to suggest why they were so adept at horse riding. Perhaps the clue lies in the close proximity of the Trysts, where mounted men would have been 'cowboys', helping to herd the cattle Less surprising is the inclusion in the Falkirk Dozen of men with surnames like Livingston, Callender and Scott – all of which appear in the local annals of warfare, notably for participating in the Battle of Preston in 1648.

The men who returned to Falkirk were honoured by their fellow townsmen and must have found it difficult to return to the humdrum of daily life after the frantic scramble to save Europe. No doubt they spent many a day in telling and re-telling stories of this major historical event, and proudly wore their Waterloo Medals on appropriate occasions. Sir John Kincaid, a Bothkennar man, whose horse was shot from under him at Waterloo, was commemorated on a stone in Falkirk Parish churchyard (though not buried there). He left one of the best contemporary accounts of the battle and was one of the most famous authors of the day. It is therefore surprising to find that, although still talked about almost a century later, the details of the 13 have almost been lost. In 1908 a questioner to the *Falkirk Herald* asked if any of the 'aulder bairns' had heard the traditional story. Thankfully, James Love responded but could give information on Thomas Nicol and James Masterton only. Hopefully the balance is redressed a little in this volume.

Biographical Notes
on the
Officers and Men
Who Served with the Scots Greys at Waterloo

Six troops of the Scots Greys, commanded by Lieutenant Colonel James Inglis Hamilton, embarked at Gravesend for Flanders in April 1815. They arrived at Ostend where they later joined the Royal and the Inniskilling Dragoons to form the Union Brigade. The six troops were captained respectively by:

1. Captain C.L. Barnard
2. Captain E. Payne
3. Captain E. Cheney
4. Captain J. Poole
5. Captain R. Vernor
6. Captain T.C. Fenton

There were about 70 men in each troop, making 444 personnel, plus 14 Staff Officers, whose details appear in the following biographical section. The names included are those that appear on the Muster Roll (National Archives, WO12/522) taken in Belgium which covers 18th June 1815, the date of the battle of Waterloo. Those names that appear on the Muster prior to the battle, but not afterwards, have been checked against available casualty rolls for more details (killed in action, died of wounds &cc). The rank shown with each person's name is that held at the time of the battle of Waterloo, although, where possible, any subsequent promotion(s) (and demotion(s)) are recorded in the biographical notes. Some men changed troop after Waterloo, often because it was necessary to supplement an especially depleted troop, or because a promotion occurred.

Details of officers have been extracted from a number of sources – printed regimental histories, such as Almack and Cannon, manuscript records at the National Archives, such as WO25 (Officers Returns), and Officers Memoranda (WO31); and occasionally from private letters written by officers to family and colleagues (where possible these are cited individually). Officers who signed for Waterloo prize money (see list in Almack, 1908) have this detail recorded in their biographies as this confirms active participation in the Waterloo campaign. Unfortunately, Almack did not publish the details of prize money apportioned to other ranks.

The main source of information about rank and file troops is the WO 97 series of Chelsea discharge papers (National Archives). These give place of birth, previous occupation, brief physical description (hair, eye colour and height – height was an important factor in the selection of recruits for the Regiment). Relevant comments about a man's service and conduct were usually recorded by the officer in attendance at the time of discharge, often this was the Commanding Officer. The date and reason for discharge were also stated, and verified by the Regiment's Medical Officer.

Between July 1818–21, the Scots Greys were stationed in Ireland, hence several men were discharged to pension through Kilmainham Hospital and their discharge papers have also been used as sources of information (National Archives, WO118). Occasionally private letters have been of use and are cited.

At the risk of being repetitious, it is noted in the biographies if the officers and men appear NOT to have received injuries at Waterloo simply to emphasise the fact that every effort has been made to ascertain such information as incontrovertible proof that the individual definitely participated in the battle of Waterloo. It should be remembered that some injuries (such as falling from a horse) may not have occurred in battle and need further investigation. Most of the 458 individuals listed on the Waterloo Muster Roll, and whose names follow here, would have participated in the Union Brigade Charge and the battle of Waterloo, but a few would not (some would have been attending the horses, or perhaps were sick themselves &cc), so only by providing evidence that an individual was a battle casualty, received prize money, is noted in an eyewitness account &cc, can this be proven beyond any doubt whatsoever.

Note

*   Finally, it is important to know that soldiers were credited with two years additional service for being with the Regiment at Waterloo. This would have applied to any of those listed. However, only when there is an actual record of this, have the two years have been added to the length of service shown in individual biographies and this is indicated by an asterisk* against the relevant names.

Staff Officers

Major General Sir William PONSONBY

Born, 1772, he was the second son of the First Baron Ponsonby of Imokilly, co Cork. Married 1807, Georgiana Fitzroy, daughter of Charles Fitzroy, First Baron Southampton.

Took command of the 5th Dragoon Guards 1803 and served in Spain 1811-14. Fought at Salamanca 1812 and took command of Le Marchant's Brigade after the latter was killed. As a result, he was awarded a small Army Gold Medal for Salamanca. Later led his own Brigade at Vittoria and was awarded a Large Gold Medal for Vittoria 1813 with bar Salamanca. Awarded a K.C.B. in 1815.

Commanded the Union Brigade at Waterloo and was later killed in the battle by French Lancers. His remains were placed in the family vault at Kensington. There is no record of Ponsonby being awarded a Waterloo Medal, although it would be surprising to find that members of his family were unaware that, as he was a casualty, they had to apply for the award.

Major of Brigade Thomas REIGNOLDS

Appointed Cornet, 23rd November 1797; soon promoted Lieutenant; Captain, 11th April, 1805; Major, June 1814. Killed alongside General William Ponsonby by French Lancers at Waterloo. His death may have been hastened by the delay and diversion created by Ponsonby who attempted to pass to Reignolds a snuff box and miniature portrait of the former's wife.

Lieutenant Colonel James Inglis HAMILTON

Born Jamie Anderson, July 1777, Tayantroga, America. Father, Sergeant Major Anderson, 21st Foot, who had served under the then Colonel James Inglis Hamilton in America. Hamilton became a Major General and later, by chance, met former Sergeant Anderson whilst visiting Glasgow. The latter introduced his son, Jamie. The old General was impressed and supported Jamie with his education at Glasgow Grammar School. General Hamilton had no heir, so he adopted Jamie who then became known as James Inglis Hamilton. Subsequently obtaining a commission in the 2nd Dragoons, Jamie's career went from strength to strength supported by General Hamilton.

Cornet, May 1793; Lieutenant, October 1793; Captain, 1800; Major, 1803; Lieutenant Colonel, 1807; Colonel, June 1814.

At Waterloo he displayed great courage, if not prudence, leading his men in action almost to annihilation. Colonel Hamilton had both his arms cut off in the charge, but carried on with the reins between his teeth. His body was found on the field with evidence of several wounds and a musket ball through the heart. The scabbard and silken sash worn by James Hamilton were retrieved and given to his brother Lieutenant John Anderson, who died 1816 from wounds he had received at Salamanca 1812. These relics were donated by the Hamilton sisters to the National Museum of Scotland 1888.

Captain Payne was informed by Colonel Hamilton's servant of the possessions which had been taken from his master These included: one pistol, one cloak , one valise, one swordbelt, one dressing gown, one pair of overalls, two pairs of drawers, three pairs of socks, two silk handkerchiefs, 33 white cravats. The value of these items was not stated.

In 1880, a memorial tablet to Lieutenant Colonel Inglis Hamilton was erected in Kirk O'Shotts church, near Salsburgh, Lanarkshire by officers of the Scots Greys. The family home is Murdostoun Castle. Seemingly two Waterloo Medals were issued to this courageous officer – perhaps it would have been fitting if one had been named to him in the name of Anderson.

Waterloo Medal extant, National War Museum Scotland.

Major Isaac Blake CLARKE

Cornet, 1795; Lieutenant, 1796; Captain, 7th September 1797; Major, 16th June 1807; Brevet Colonel, 1813; Lieutenant Colonel, 20th July 1815.

Served in Flanders, then present at the battle of Waterloo. During the battle, he took command of the Regiment after the death of Lieutenant Colonel Inglis Hamilton. He then relinquished command to Captain Cheney, when he was wounded himself.

In a later address to the Regiment (see page 44), the then Colonel Clarke displayed good leadership skills by congratulating the Waterloo Medal recipients but, at the same time, not ignoring those men who did not receive the award. In so doing, he recognised the valuable and important work of the other four companies left behind in England. Doubtless his words reduced resentment and aided esprit de corps.

Awarded the CB in 1816 for his services at Waterloo. The Russian Order of St Anne (2nd Class) was conferred on him for gallantry at Waterloo. Also received prize money for Waterloo. The British Headquarters in Paris received a supplementary despatch in October 1815 stating that Colonel Clarke had been given the award by the Emperor of Russia (Carlisle, 1839). Retired 11th October 1821; died at St Peters, Isle of Thanet, 7th January 1850, age 76. Buried in St James Church, Broadstairs.

Waterloo Medal extant, private collection.

Major Thomas Pate HANKIN

Ensign, 22nd July 1795; Lieutenant, 3rd August 1796; Captain, October 1798; Major, 4th April 1808; Brevet Lieutenant Colonel, 4th June 1814. Present at the battle of Waterloo, but he did not take part in the charge. He was thrown from his horse when it reared at the sound of an exploding shell. Received prize money for Waterloo.

Knighted by the Prince Regent, 1816. Died at Norwich, 20th October 1825, age 59. A memorial tablet was erected to him in Norwich Cathedral. Married Sarah Reade, no children as Sarah died during her first pregnancy.

Surgeon Robert DAUN

Enlisted, age 18 as a hospital mate, 1803. Then employed as Assistant Surgeon, 59th Foot and 25th Dragoons. Obtained an MD at Kings College, 1813.

Transferred to the 2nd Dragoons, August 1814, as Surgeon. Exchanged to 89 Foot, 1817. Discharged on Half Pay, 1832 and went to live in Aberdeen. Died, 14th June 1871.

Waterloo Medal extant, Regimental Museum.

Assistant Surgeon James ALEXANDER

Enlisted, as a hospital mate, 1811. Joined 2nd Dragoons as Assistant Surgeon, January 1812. Served in the Waterloo campaign. Later transferred to 28 Foot; Half Pay, 1st March 1821.

Veterinary Surgeon John TRIGG

Joined Scots Grey, 1807. Received prize money for Waterloo. In 1815, the Veterinary Department of the Army was 19 years old. Two months before Waterloo an Order stated that officers with less than 10 years experience should be given the rank of Cornet, those with more than 10 years should be Lieutenants (these ranks did not allow military command).

Paymaster William DAWSON

Joined, October 1814. Received prize money for Waterloo. It has not been possible to find any evidence to suggest he rode in the charge.

Died, September 1828.

Waterloo Medal extant (Provenance: Dix Noonan Webb 2005).

Adjutant Lieutenant Henry MacMILLAN

Joined Regiment, 1786; rose through the ranks, promoted from Sergeant Major to Adjutant, 1st October 1802; Lieutenant, April 1805; Captain, 18 July 1815 after the death of Captain Reignolds. Served in three European campaigns, 1793, 1794 and 1795.

A letter (Almack, page 71), from MacMillan to Major General Balfour, Balburnie, Fife, describes the action at Waterloo and the fate of some of his comrades. He described participating in the charge at Waterloo and how, luckily, he avoided the musket balls, despite his cloak being holed several times by near misses. However, his horse was not so fortunate, sustaining a musket ball wound to the shoulder. He confirmed that Clarke's horse was killed and the rider wounded, also that Poole and Vernor encountered similar difficulties. Furthermore Cheney's loss of five horses did not go unnoticed. MacMillan expressed deep regret that Carruthers died on 19th June of his wounds. Some men, regrettably, received wounds after being taken prisoner which resulted in the rumour that the French were not taking prisoners. The letter concluded with the statement that he expected Major Clarke to be promoted to Colonel. Received prize money for Waterloo.

MacMillan lived in Kirkcaldy from 1817.

Waterloo Medal extant, Dr John Cruickshank collection.

Lieutenant James CARRUTHERS

From an old landed family in Annandale, Dumfriesshire. The clan Carruthers was related to the Bruces and this entitled them to wear the Bruce tartan.

Cornet by purchase, 1811; Lieutenant, February 1815. Died of wounds at Waterloo. Dickson, in his account, mentioned that he was saddened to see Carruthers lying injured and regretted he could not stop because he was being pursued by French Lancers.

Lieutenant Thomas TROTTER

Born, 27th September 1795, son of Lieutenant General Alexander Trotter of Morton Hall, Midlothian. Joined 3rd Regiment of Dragoons as Cornet, 1812; served in the Peninsula wars. In a letter to his mother (in family archive), he describes narrowly escaping death at the battle of Toulouse, 1814: 'A musket ball whistled past my ear, killing the rider by my side'.

Trotter arrived at Waterloo without any equipment. An injured private, Robert Stirling, gave the young officer his sword, belt and pistol. He was killed in action by a French officer after the first charge, as witnessed by Corporal Dickson. On the day after Waterloo, his body was buried on the battlefield with other Scots Grey officers.

In a letter, to Captain Lawson from Lieutenant A. J. Hamilton (Almack, page 69) confirmed that Trotter was shot through the heart. Hamilton also said that he would manage Trotter's affairs and send any money left to the family. Some of Trotter's personal effects are in the Regimental Museum, including his telescope and a spoon. His Waterloo Medal is believed to be in the possession of the Trotter family.

Cornet Lemuel SHULDHAM

Born, 27th February 1794. The younger of two sons, born to William and Mary Shuldham of Marlesford, Suffolk. Joined the Regiment, 19th January 1815, therefore was one of the least experienced officers, which undoubtedly contributed to his death as he got separated from his troop during the charge at Waterloo. Buried on the field by members of the Regiment under the supervision of Lieutenant Graham.

A memorial plaque to Cornet Shuldham exists in the parish church of Marlesford (*see below*).

Cornet Edward WESTBY

Third son of William Westby, Thornhill, Dublin. Killed in action at Waterloo where his death was witnessed by Lieutenant John Mills who stated in a letter that Edward died at the hands of the French Lancers. It seems likely that Westby was the last of the three Cornets to die and he did so towards the end of the action. His memorial is in St. Peter's Church, Dublin.

CHOMAS CROTTER
The ROYAL SCOTS GREYS.

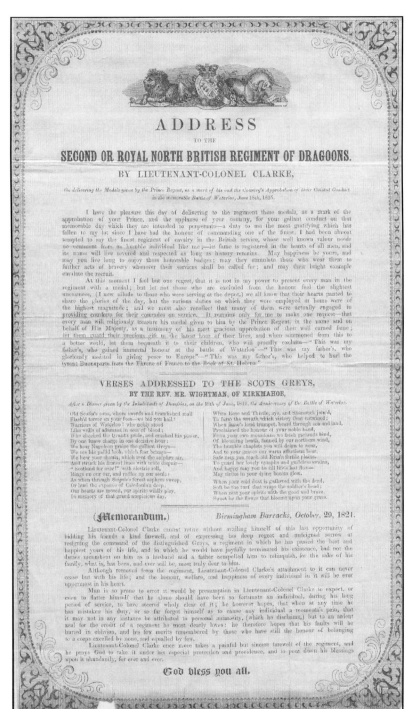

The origins of this document relating to Lieutenant Colonel I.B. Clarke is unclear

(in the author's collection)

Nelly – the horse ridden by Lieutenant MacMillan at Waterloo, painted in 1830 by David Dalby (1794–1836) of York, when the horse was well into her twenties. Traditionally it hangs over the fireplace in the Officers Mess of the Scots Greys. It states on the picture that she was the fourth mount of Adjutant Henry MacMillan.

Barnard's Troop

Captain Charles Levyns BARNARD

Second son of Henry Barnard, Cave Castle, Yorkshire. Formerly 38 Foot, served in the campaigns in Germany and nearly the whole of the Peninsula wars; severely wounded at the storming of Badajoz 1812.

Captain, Scots Greys, February 1815. Killed in action at Waterloo, age 25 years, where he led the right squadron of his Regiment into action before he fell. Displayed talent and courage that gained him the admiration of his brother officers. An epitaph to this courageous officer in the church at South Cave reads:

'This tablet is erected to the memory of Capt Charles Levyns Barnard of the 2nd R N B Dragoons who died at Waterloo 18 June 1815 aged 25 years and was buried on the field of battle. Ye that respect the union of virtue, valour and ability pause ere you may pass this tablet, and if you have sons or brothers Pray that their lives may be as fair, and their deaths as glorious as his'.

Lieutenant George Home FALCONER

Cornet, November 1809; Lieutenant, 21st November 1811; Half Pay, 25th March 1816. May have been on baggage guard at Brussels at the time of Waterloo; this fact is supported by the omission of his name from the list of officers who received Waterloo prize money (Almack). Died Woodcot, co Haddington, 15th September 1820.

Waterloo Medal extant (Provenance: Ambrose Elson collection 1963).

Troop Sergeant Major William PERRIE

Born, Kilmarnock; a weaver by trade. Enlisted, 25th August 1794. Appears not to have sustained any injuries at Waterloo.

Waterloo Medal extant (Provenance: London Stamp Exchange 1985).

Regimental Sergeant Major William CRAWFORD

Born, Edinburgh, February 1784. Enlisted, 1799; Corporal, 1801; Regimental Sergeant Major at Waterloo; Cornet, August 1815; Lieutenant, 1819; Paymaster for 20 years until 1849. Served 32 years with the Regiment. In his Waterloo letters, Lieutenant A.J. Hamilton states that this Sergeant particularly distinguished himself. Crawford himself confirmed that at Waterloo the Greys reached the high ground and sabred the French gunners and drivers but were unable to remove the guns which they had captured.

Paymaster Sergeant William BAYNE

Born, Perth; a gardener by trade. Enlistment height, 5ft 8ins. Appears not to have sustained any injuries at Waterloo. Served 24 years with the Regiment. Discharged through Chelsea Pension office due to being worn out. His general conduct was described as very good.

Waterloo Medal extant (Provenance: Dix Noonan Webb 2002).

Armourer Sergeant James BRAY

Enlisted, June 1813, age 23 years. Appears not to have sustained any injuries at Waterloo.

Saddler Sergeant Alexander WALLACE*

Born, Mauchlin, Ayr; a saddler by trade. Enlistment height, 5ft 9ins. Appears not to have sustained any injuries at Waterloo. Served 23 years with the Regiment. Discharged due to being worn out.

Waterloo Medal extant (Provenance: Oakley collection 1953).

Sergeant John GILLIES*

Born, Dunse, Berwick; a weaver by trade. Enlisted, 1793; height, 5ft 8ins. He was wounded in action in 1793. Appears not to have sustained any injuries at Waterloo. Later Troop Sergeant Major. Served 26 years with the Regiment. Discharged through Chelsea Pension office, 1817, due to an affliction of the head, which nearly destroyed his hearing and debility. His general conduct was described as extremely good.

Waterloo Medal extant (Provenance: Glendining 1981).

Sergeant Arthur POLLOCK

Born, Blantyre; a weaver by trade. Killed in action at Waterloo.

Sergeant William PORTEOUS*

Born, Stenten, Haddington; a labourer by trade. Enlisted, 1794; height, 6ft 1in. Badly wounded at Waterloo, receiving 8 lance wounds to different parts of his body. His wounds were treated at Brussels between June and September 1815. Served 13 years with the Regiment. Discharged through Chelsea Pension office, October 1816, due to a damaged elbow joint sustained at Waterloo. His conduct report described him as a worthy good man.

Waterloo Medal extant (Provenance: Buckland Dix & Wood).

Sergeant John WHITE*

Born, Renfrew; a sawyer by trade. Enlisted, 1799; height, 5ft 10ins. Appears not to have sustained any injuries at Waterloo. Served 28 years with the Regiment, 17 of them as a sergeant. Discharged through Chelsea Pension office, 1826, due to being worn out. His general conduct was described as very good.

Corporal Alexander HALL*

Born, Inveresk, Musselburgh; a blacksmith by trade. Served one year in the West Lothian Fencible Cavalry prior to joining the Scots Greys. Enlisted, 1800; height, 5ft 8ins. Appears not to have sustained any injuries at Waterloo. Served 11 years with the Regiment. Discharged through Chelsea Pension office, 1821, due to a liver complaint. His general conduct was described as very good.

Corporal Alexander LYNCH (LITCH)

Enlisted, January 1806. His surname may have been Litch. Appears not to have sustained any injuries at Waterloo.

Corporal John SCOTT

Born, Hamilton, Lanark; a weaver by trade. Enlisted, 1810; height, 6ft 1in. Wounded severely in the right leg at Waterloo, which was amputated above the knee. Sent with the wounded to Brussels. Served five years with the Regiment. Discharged at Rouen through Chelsea Pension office, October 1815, as a consequence of wounds. His general conduct was described as good.

Corporal Hugh WYLIE

Born, 16th August 1790. Enlisted, November 1807. Appears not to have sustained any injuries at Waterloo.

Trumpeter Humphrey STEVENSON

Enlisted, 11th March 1794. Appears not to have sustained any injuries at Waterloo.

Private John AITKIN

Enlisted, March 1800; a labourer by trade. Enlistment height, 5ft 11ins. Previously served in the Lanark Fencibles, 1799-1800. Appears not to have sustained any injuries at Waterloo. Served 18 years with the Regiment. Discharged through Kilmainham Pension office, 1818, due to chronic rheumatism and headaches.

Private John ANDREWS*

Born, Glasgow; a labourer by trade. Enlisted, 1804; height, 5ft 7ins. Sustained a severe contusion of his breast, after falling from his horse at Riding School, 1809. Appears not to have sustained any injuries at Waterloo. Served 17 years with the Regiment. Discharged through Chelsea Pension office, October 1821. His general conduct was described as good.

Private James BALLANTYNE*

Born, Ayr; a labourer by trade. Enlistment height, 5ft 7ins. Appears not to have sustained any injuries at Waterloo. Served six years with the Regiment. Discharged through Chelsea Pension office, 1818, due to reduction of the Regiment. His general conduct was described as good.

Waterloo Medal extant, private collection.

Private Edward BELL*

Born, Kirkmichael, Ayr; a labourer by trade. Enlisted, May 1799; height, 5ft 7ins. Served 24 years with the Regiment. Discharged through Chelsea Pension office, October 1821, having lost the power in his left arm from an injury sustained in 1821, which rendered him unfit for further service. He was described as a clean, very good soldier

Private Isaac BELL

Born, 29th June 1798. Enlisted, 2nd February 1814. Transferred from the Depot to the Regiment in Belgium, 17th May 1815. Appears not to have sustained any injuries at Waterloo.

Private Alexander BLACK

Born, Dunfermline; a weaver by trade. Killed in action at Waterloo.

Private John BLAIN

Born, Ayr, Blain; a weaver by trade. Enlisted, December 1797; height, 5ft 8ins. Served 20 years with the Regiment. Discharged due to rheumatism and asthma.

Private William BRINSBY (BRIMSLY)

Born, Horton; a labourer by trade. Name also recorded as Baisby on Almack's Roll of Honour. Killed in action at Waterloo.

Private William BROMLEY

Born, 21st May 1797. Enlisted, January 1814. Appears not to have sustained any injuries at Waterloo.

Private James BULLOCK*

Born, St. Margarets, Norwich; a bricklayer by trade. Enlistment height, 5ft 8ins. Appears not to have sustained any injuries at Waterloo. Served 19 years with the Regiment. Discharged through Chelsea Pension office, September 1822, due to chronic rheumatism and being worn out. His general conduct was described as good

Waterloo Medal extant (Provenance: Glendining 1987).

Private John CALLENDER

Born, Falkirk, Stirling; a baker by trade. Enlisted, 1813; height, 5ft 10ins. Appears not to have sustained any injuries at Waterloo. Served 25 years with the Regiment. Discharged through Chelsea Pension office, June 1838, due to chronic rheumatism and pulmonary disability. His general conduct was described as remarkably good.

A baker of this name lived at Kirk Wynd in 1841. At that date he was aged 60, which would have made him 34 at the battle of Waterloo. Callander was one of the celebrated Falkirk 13.

Private John CHAMBLING
Born, Biggleswade, Bedford; a labourer by trade. Enlisted, December 1804; height, 5ft 9ins. Appears not to have sustained any injuries at Waterloo. Discharged through Chelsea Pension office, due to deafness and a pulmonary complaint. His general conduct was described as tolerable and it was noted that he was an active soldier.

Private James CLACHAN
Born, Toon, Ayr; a wright by trade. Enlisted, August 1805; height, 5ft 8ins. Served 22 years with the Regiment. Discharged due to being worn out.

Private John DOUGAL
Born, Barony, Glasgow; a labourer by trade. Enlisted, 15th February 1813. Died, 13th July 1815, due to wounds sustained at Waterloo.

Private James DRUMMOND*
Born, Paisley, Glasgow; a turner by trade. Enlisted, April 1812; height, 5ft 8ins. Appears not to have sustained any injuries at Waterloo. Served 19 years with the Regiment. Discharged through Chelsea Pension office, May 1829, due to consumption (tuberculosis). His general conduct was described as good.

Private George FIDDES
Enlisted, December 1806. Wounded at Waterloo. At Brussels recovering from his wounds, September 1815.

Private James FRAME*
Born, Hamilton, Lanark; a wright by trade. Enlisted, February 1804; height, 5ft 9ins. Appears not to have sustained any injuries at Waterloo. Served 20 years with the Regiment. Discharged through Chelsea Pension office, February 1823, due to being worn out with chronic rheumatism. His general conduct was described as good.
Waterloo Medal extant (Provenance: Glendining 1939, EE Needes collection).

Private James GIBSON*
Born, Kilmarnock, Ayr; a weaver by trade. Enlisted, March 1806; height, 5ft 7ins. Appears not to have sustained any injuries at Waterloo. Served 17 years with the Regiment. Discharged through Chelsea Pension office, 1821, due to chronic affection (*sic*) of the spleen since 1818. His general conduct was described as very good and remarkably clean.

Private Alexander GREY
Born, Paisley; a weaver by trade. His name is recorded as Gray on Almack's Roll of Honour. Killed in action at Waterloo.

Private Henry HEAD*

Born, Shoreham, Canterbury, Kent; a labourer by trade. Enlisted, June 1803; height, 5ft 8ins. Appears not to have sustained any injuries at Waterloo. Served 24 years with the Regiment. Discharged through Chelsea Pension office, April 1826, due to being worn out. His general conduct was described as good.

Private John JAMISON

Born, Barony, Glasgow; a labourer by trade. Killed in action at Waterloo.

Private John JARVIE

Enlisted, November 1805. Appears not to have sustained any injuries at Waterloo.

Private Joseph JARVIE

Born, Kilsyth, Stirling; a weaver by trade. Enlistment height, 5ft 7ins. Served 20 years with the Regiment. Discharged due to chronic rheumatism and being worn out.

Private David KELLY (KALLY)

Born, Chuchinbrick, Kirkcudbright; a currier [sic] by trade. His surname may have been Kally. Enlisted, October 1810. Severely wounded at Waterloo. He was sent to Brussels to recover from his wound and then returned to England. Served for over five years with the Regiment and for 2 months with the 5th Royal Veteran Battalion. Discharged through Chelsea Pension office, 18th January 1816, as severe wounds rendered him unfit for service.

Waterloo Medal extant (Provenance: Glendining 1919).

Private Alexander KERR

Born, Ayr; a blacksmith by trade. Killed in action at Waterloo.

Private John KIDD

Born, Kinross; a labourer by trade. Killed in action at Waterloo.

Private William KIDD

Enlisted, June 1808. Sent to Brussels to recover from wounds sustained at Waterloo.

Private James KNOX

Enlisted, April 1803; a labourer by trade. Appears not to have sustained any injuries at Waterloo. Discharged through Kilmainham Pension office, 1818, due to leg ulcers.

Private John LIVINGSTON*

Born, Falkirk, Stirling; a baker by trade. Enlisted, 1806; height, 5ft 8ins. Served 17 years with the Regiment. Discharged through Chelsea Pension office, 23 October 1821, due to being unfit after sustaining a contusion of his breast at Waterloo when his dead horse fell on him. His general conduct was described as good. Livingston was a member of the celebrated Falkirk 13.

Private William LUKE*
Born, Alnwick, Northumberland; a labourer by trade. Enlisted, September 1805; height, 5ft 11ins. Appears not to have sustained any injuries at Waterloo. Served 22 years with the Regiment. Discharged through Chelsea Pension office, 11 October 1825, due to an organic heart condition. His general conduct was described as very good.

Private Robert MacKIE
Born, Blantyre; a labourer by trade. Killed in action at Waterloo.

Private Adam McCREE (MCCRIE)
Enlisted, April 1811. His surname may have been McCrie. Appears not to have sustained any injuries at Waterloo.

Private Andrew McFARLAN
Born, Glasgow; a painter by trade. Killed in action at Waterloo.

Private James McFARLAN
Enlisted, Glasgow, March 1814. Killed in action at Waterloo.

Private Daniel McKECHNEY
Born, Greenock; a butcher by trade. Killed in action at Waterloo.

Private James McMILLAN*
Born, Barony, Glasgow; a weaver by trade. Enlisted, September 1793; height, 5ft 8ins. After Waterloo, he attended the wounded horses at Brussels. Appears not to have sustained any injuries at Waterloo. Served 26 years with the Regiment. Discharged through Chelsea Pension office, January 1818, due to being worn out with defective vision. His general conduct was described as extremely good.

Private John MARSHALL*
Born, Little Compton, Moreton on Marsh, Gloucester; a labourer by trade. Enlisted, March 1805; height, 5ft 7ins. Appears not to have sustained any injuries at Waterloo. Served 26 years with the Regiment. Discharged through Chelsea Pension office, July 1830, due to mental imbecility and a broken down constitution, he suffered from paralysis agitans (neuro-syphilis). His general conduct was described as unacceptable for a soldier.

Private Robert MATHEWS
Born, Sutton, Nottinghamshire; a labourer by trade. Enlisted, September 1805; height, 5ft 8ins. Appears not to have sustained any injuries at Waterloo. Served 14 years with the Regiment. Discharged through

Chelsea Pension office, August 1818, due to incontinence of urine and chronic rheumatism. He was described as a very clean soldier.

Private David MATHIE*

Born, Kilmarnock, Ayr; a weaver by trade. Enlisted, October 1804; height, 5ft 8ins. Appears not to have sustained any injuries at Waterloo. Served 24 years with the Regiment. Discharged through Chelsea Pension office, 1826, due to being worn out. His general conduct was described as very good.

Waterloo Medal extant (Provenance: Bostock Militaria 2006).

Private Hugh MERRIE

Enlisted, Glasgow, May 1805. Killed in action at Waterloo.

Private John MILLAR

Born, Old Monkland, Lanarkshire; a weaver by trade. Killed in action at Waterloo.

Private John (James) NAIRN

Enlisted, June 1798. His forename may have been James. Appears not to have sustained any injuries at Waterloo. After Waterloo, he transferred to No. 2 Troop.

Private Thomas NICOL

Born, Falkirk, 1791, son of Thomas Nicol, sawyer, and Mary Miller; a baker by trade. Enlisted, 1807, age 17 years. Tam', as he was known, was described as athletic, healthy and 5ft 10ins. At Waterloo, Nicol was heavily involved in the fighting and sustained severe wounds. During the battle he was unhorsed and, whilst lying on the ground, his leg trapped beneath his horse, three French Lancers struck him several times and left him for dead. He was rescued by a 6th Dragoon called Maxwell, who became his friend whilst they were in hospital at Brussels recovering from their wounds. In fact, Nicol was hospitalised for six weeks whilst the deep wounds healed in his thigh, back and shoulder. Survived the wounds. Discharged through Kilmainham Pension office, November 1828, due to severe concussion sustained whilst on duty, May 1827. Received a pension of 18 pence a day.

He returned to his native town of Falkirk, Stirlingshire, and was employed as a groom at Callander House. Married Sophie Moody, by whom he had a daughter and three sons, the last when he was in his 50s. Later became porter to a merchant, James Rankine. Died in Wooer's Close after a long illness, 1862, age 71 years. Buried in Falkirk Parish churchyard. He was the last survivor of the celebrated Falkirk 13.

Private William PATRICK

Born, Kilmarnock, Ayrshire; a baker by trade. Enlisted, July 1810; Corporal, October 1815; Sergeant, 1821. Appears not to have sustained any injuries at Waterloo. Reported as sick at Chantilly, July 1815. Served 25 years with the Regiment. Discharged through Chelsea Pension office, August 1831, due to cicatrices (scars) on the back of his left leg which damaged the nerve – injuries sustained in Edinburgh, 1826. His general conduct was described as very good.

Private David PENTLAND

Enlisted, April 1807. Appears not to have sustained any injuries at Waterloo.

Private David PICKEN

Born, Stewarton, Ayrshire; a weaver by trade. Killed in action at Waterloo.

Private William PROVAN*

Born, Barony, Glasgow; a callenderer by trade. Joined Perth Fencibles, 1799; served with 28th Light Dragoons 1800-1802. Enlistment height, 5ft 8ins. Some time after Waterloo he transferred to No. 5 Troop. Served 13 years with the Regiment. Discharged through Chelsea Pension office, 1816, due an ulcerated left leg, sustained in June 1815. He was described as a clean, good soldier.

Waterloo Medal extant (Provenance: Christie 1990).

Private John RAYBURN

Born, Paisley; a weaver by trade. Killed in action at Waterloo.

Private John ROBERTSON

Born, Paisley; a weaver by trade. Enlisted, November 1809. Killed in action at Waterloo.

Private William ROBERTSON*

Born, Hamilton, Lanark; a weaver by trade. Enlisted, February 1807; height, 5ft 9ins. Appears not to have sustained any injuries at Waterloo. Served 22 years with the Regiment. Discharged through Chelsea Pension office, May 1829, due to damaged left ankle. His general conduct was described as good.

Private Job ROOD*

Born, Wootton, Leicestershire; a stocking weaver by trade. Enlisted, October 1797; height, 5ft 8ins. Appears not to have sustained any injuries at Waterloo. Served 31 years with the Regiment. Discharged through Chelsea Pension office, May 1827, due to being worn out. His general conduct was described as good.

Private James ROWAN*

Born, Glasgow; a weaver by trade. Enlisted, March 1793; height, 5ft 7ins. Appears not to have sustained any injuries at Waterloo. Served 26 years with the Regiment. Discharged through Chelsea Pension office, January 1818, due to being worn out. His general conduct was described as extremely good, a most excellent soldier who had never been in confinement during his long service.

Private John SAWERS

Born, Rutherglen, Lanarkshire; a dyer by trade. Killed in action at Waterloo.

Private William TAYLOR

Born, Freckingham, Suffolk; a shoemaker by trade. Enlistment height, 5ft 7ins. Wounded at Waterloo, once in the neck, six times in the left arm, twice in the left side and also in the left thigh, and was sent to Brussels to recover. Served 14 years with the Regiment. Discharged through Chelsea Pension office, August 1818. His general conduct was described as very good. Later served one year seven months with the 7th Veteran Battalion until 1821.

Private Robert TENNANT

Born, Dewny; a weaver by trade. Killed in action at Waterloo.

Private John WATSON

Born, Glenholm, Peebles; a labourer by trade. Enlisted, October 1804. Appears not to have sustained any injuries at Waterloo. Served 23 years with the Regiment. Discharged through Chelsea Pension office, due to being worn out. His general conduct was described as very good.

Private Robert WATT

Enlisted, March 1811. Appears not to have sustained any injuries at Waterloo.

Private William WELLS

With the Fifeshire Fencible Cavalry, 1st November 1799 to 8th March 1800. Enlisted, 9th March 1800. Sent to Brussels to recover from wounds sustained at Waterloo.

Private John WHITE*

Born, Shaftesbury; a shoemaker by trade. Enlisted, March 1803; height, 5ft 9ins. Appears not to have sustained any injuries at Waterloo. Served 15 years with the Regiment. Discharged through Chelsea Pension office, 1816, due to palsy of the legs and general weakness. He was described as a good steady man.

Private William WILLIAMSON*

Born, Hamilton; a weaver by trade. Enlisted, February 1798; height, 5ft 8ins. Appears not to have sustained any injuries at Waterloo. Served for 26 years with the Regiment. Discharged through Chelsea Pension office, February 1823, due to being worn out and afflicted by rheumatism. His general conduct was described as very good.

Private David WILSON

Enlisted, February 1806. Appears not to have sustained any injuries at Waterloo.

Private Thomas YOUNG

Enlisted, October 1804. Appears not to have sustained any injuries at Waterloo.

Payne's Troop

Captain Edward PAYNE
Cornet, 17th March 1807; Lieutenant, 13th October 1808; Captain by purchase, 5th April 1815. One of only two senior officers, the other being Cheney, not to be wounded at Waterloo . Later resigned and went to live in Broadwater Farm, near Worthing. His Waterloo Medal was recorded as being sent there, 1st April 1816. Captain Payne does not appear on the list of officers entitled to a share of the Waterloo prize money, however he had left the Regiment in 1817.

Waterloo Medal extant, private collection (Provenance: Glendining 1993).

Lieutenant Archibald James HAMILTON
Born, October 1793. Son of General John Hamilton, Dalzell. Cornet, 4th Dragoons, January 1812, age 18 years; Lieutenant by purchase, June 1812. Served in the Peninsula with 4th Light Dragoons. Appointed Lieutenant, 2nd Dragoons, March 1815. Wounded at Waterloo.

Served as an Aide to Major General Ponsonby with whom he had previously served in Spain. Hamilton just escaped death at the hands of Polish Lancers when Ponsonby and Reignolds were killed. He attributed his lucky escape to having a better horse than his less fortunate comrades. After Waterloo, he purchased Lieutenant Colonel Hamilton's favourite horse for the very reasonable price, so he considered, of 55 pounds.

Married, 16th January 1827, at Edgcott Church, Northants. Died, January 1834.

Waterloo Medal extant, private collection (Provenance: J.B. Hayward & Son).

Lieutenant Charles WYNDHAM
Born, London, 1795. Cornet, 10th Light Dragoons, 17th October 1811; Lieutenant, 5th November 1812. Served in the Peninsular War, and fought at Vittoria, Orthes, Torbes, and Toulouse. Wounded at Espinasse, 4th April 1814. Transferred to Scots Greys as Lieutenant, May 1815; Captain, 1819; Major, 1826; Lieutenant Colonel by purchase, 1837. Twice wounded at Waterloo; one wound in the left foot. He wrote letters to Siborne (1891), in which he gives an account of the action and confirms being wounded.

Between 1826-27, Wyndham put his equestrian skills to good use in the Leicestershire hunting season. A former charger at Waterloo, he was a very powerful man, weighing no less than 16 stone. This strength was put to good use and no fence ever stopped him – those he could not get over, he went through, making a gap large enough for a regiment to follow. A fox had little chance of escape with Wyndham in hot pursuit (Wilmot, 1859).

Later appointed Keeper of the Crown Jewels, Tower of London, where he served for 20 years.

Died, 15th February 1872, age 76 years, at Traitor's Gate, Tower of London, due to hemiplegia (stroke) for 18 months and bronchitis for 7 days. He was the longest surviving Waterloo officer; at

A young Wyndham dismounted and wearing his Waterloo Medal

Henry, George, and Charles Wyndham, 1814. Charles Wyndham (on the right) wears the uniform of the 10th Hussars. The name of his canine friend is not known. From a painting by Sir W. Beechey.

death he is shown as Colonel (Half Pay). His funeral was attended by Corporal Dickson, the last man to survive. He was the last person to be buried in the Chapel, 1872.

Waterloo Medal extant, author's collection (Provenance: J.B. Hyward & Son). Also received a Military General Service Medal 1793–1814 with 3 clasps – Vittoria, Orthes, Toulouse – for his service in the 10th Hussars, whereabouts unknown.

Troop Sergeant Major William ROBERTSON*

Born, Renfrew; a painter by trade. Enlisted, 1794; height, 5ft 9ins. Was in every charge made by the Regiment at Waterloo. Appears not to have sustained any injuries at Waterloo. Served 27 years with the Regiment. Discharged, September 1821, as unfit following an injury to his knee, also subject to rheumatic gout and visual disturbance due to ophthalmia. His general conduct was described as most excellent in every aspect, and he behaved most gallantly at Waterloo. Died, Kirkcaldy, December 1825.

Sergeant James BULLOCK

Born, 1st January 1788. Enlisted, June 1805. Appears not to have sustained any injuries at Waterloo.

Sergeant David DUNN*

Born, Leith, Edinburgh; a labourer by trade. Enlistment height, 5ft 9ins. Served 18 years with the Regiment. Discharged, May 1817. His general conduct was described as extremely good and he is said to have displayed great gallantry at Waterloo, where he was wounded in the left leg and sustained fractured ribs from falling off two horses that were killed from under him, resulting in him spitting blood.

Waterloo Medal extant, private collection (Provenance: Buckland Dix & Wood).

Sergeant John McNEIL*

Born, Paisley, Renfrewshire; a hairdresser by trade. Enlisted, 1793, height, 5ft 8ins. Appears not to have sustained any injuries at Waterloo. Served 25 years with the Regiment. Discharged due to chronic rheumatism, October 1816. He was described as being of good character

Waterloo Medal extant (Provenance: Matthew Taylor collection).

Sergeant William SOMERVILLE

Born, Kilmadock, Perth Mill; a wright by trade. Enlistment height, 5ft 11ins. Sustained a lance wound of the left thigh at Waterloo. Served eight years with the Regiment.

Corporal George EDWARDS

Enlisted, 1st May 1807; Corporal, 2nd March 1815. Appears not to have sustained any injuries at Waterloo.

Corporal George MILWARD

Enlisted, 23rd May 1807. His surname also appears as Millward. Appears not to have sustained any injuries at Waterloo.

Corporal Michael NELSON (NEILSON)

Enlisted, October 1810. His surname also appears as Neilson. Later Quartermaster; Honorary Captain, 1859. Appears not to have sustained any injuries at Waterloo. Died, 6th September 1872.

Waterloo Medal extant, Regimental Museum.

Corporal John SCOTT

Born, Muiravonside; a labourer by trade. Killed in action at Waterloo. Possibly one of the celebrated Falkirk 13.

Trumpeter Hugh HUTCHINSON

Born, Galston; a weaver by trade. Killed in action at Waterloo. Said to be the soldier who initiated the capture of the French Eagle, which cost him and his mount their lives. His heroics to snatch the Eagle from the 45th French Regiment only appear to have come to light following Private Peter Swan's account of the action given under oath (original affidavit in the Regimental Archives). This resulted from a suggestion that the Eagle had been found on the ground, thus no act of gallantry was responsible for its capture (*The Times*, 1862). Swan gave Hutchinson the credit for the initial attempt for which he paid with his life. Sergeant Charles Ewart went on to effect the actual capture with considerable gallantry.

Private William ALDCORN

Born, Stichill; a labourer by trade. Killed in action at Waterloo.

Private David ANDERSON

Born, 10th September 1796. Enlisted, September 1813. Appears not to have sustained any injuries at Waterloo.

Waterloo Medal extant (Provenance: Glendining 1956).

Private Alexander ARMOUR

Enlisted, April 1807. Wounded and sent to Brussels to recuperate. After Waterloo, transferred to No. 5 Troop.

Private John BISHOP

Born, Bridford, Salisbury; a labourer by trade. Enlisted, 17th October 1800; height, 5ft 9ins. Appears not to have sustained any injuries at Waterloo. Served three years with the Regiment. Discharged due to a pulmonary complaint. His general conduct was described as good.

Private Alexander BORLAND*

Born, Glasford, Lanark; a weaver by trade. Served Lanark Fencible Cavalry 1795–1800. Enlisted, 1800; height, 5ft 8ins. Appears not to have sustained any injuries at Waterloo. Served 25 years. Discharged through Chelsea Pension office, August 1818, due to chronic rheumatism and being worn out. His general conduct was described as very good

Private Joseph BRAZIER*

Born, Buckingham; a sadler by trade. Enlisted, 1801; height, 5ft 8ins. Appears not to have sustained any injuries at Waterloo. Served 17 years with the Regiment. Discharged through Chelsea Pension office, 1816, due to asthma contracted on service.

Waterloo Medal extant (Provenance: Glendining 1903, EE Needes collection).

Private John BROWN

Enlisted, January 1814. Appears not to have sustained any injuries at Waterloo.

Private Thomas BULLOCK*

Born, Glasgow; a weaver by trade. Enlisted, 1800: height, 5ft 7ins. Severely wounded at Waterloo, receiving lance wounds to the face and upper left arm. Served 23 years with the Regiment. Discharged through Chelsea Pension office, October 1821, due to a pulmonary complaint. His general conduct was described as good.

Private Alexander CAMPBELL

Enlisted, August 1807. Appears not to have sustained any injuries at Waterloo. Later in Brussels attending the wounded horses.

Private Colin CAMPBELL

Enlisted, 26th August 1807. Appears not to have sustained any injuries at Waterloo. Later transferred to No. 6 Troop.

Private Robert CARMALY

Enlisted, June 1803. Appears not to have sustained any injuries at Waterloo.

Private William CLARK

Born, Kegworth; a woolcomber by trade. Enlisted, January 1795. Appears not to have sustained any injuries at Waterloo. He is noted as attending a wounded officer in Brussels.

Private William CUNNINGHAM*

Born, Dalkeith, Edinburgh; a labourer by trade. Enlisted, 1803; height, 5ft 8ins. Wounded at Waterloo; had to have his left thigh amputated. Patient at Colchester General Hospital, April 1816. Served 15 years with the Regiment. Discharged through Chelsea Pension office, December 1816.

Waterloo Medal extant (Provenance: Glendining 1977, Allison collection).

Private David DICK

Enlisted, January 1797. Appears not to have sustained any injuries at Waterloo.

Private Robert DONALDSON
Born, Barony, Glasgow; a mason by trade. Killed in action at Waterloo.

Private Henry EAVES
Enlisted, 2nd November 1805. Wounded at Waterloo, subsequently in hospital at Brussels, then invalided. Died, 1st April 1816. His Waterloo Medal is recorded as having been returned to the depot at Canterbury.

Private Peter EWENS
Born, Ayr; a labourer by trade. Enlisted, 1797; height, 5ft 8ins. Appears not to have sustained any injuries at Waterloo. Promoted Corporal. Served 21 years with the Regiment. Discharged through Chelsea Pension office, May 1817, due to pulmonic affection (*sic*) with spitting of blood and violent rheumatism. His general conduct was described as extremely good and it was noted that he had done well at Waterloo.

Private Thomas FERGUS
Born, Paisley; resided, Glasgow. Enlistment height, 5ft 10ins. Wounded in the head at Waterloo. Served 10 years with the Regiment; a late pension claimant, age 66 years, 1851.
   Waterloo Medal extent (Provenance: Baldwin 1975)

Private William FLEMING*
Born, Kilmarnock; a weaver by trade. Enlisted, 1812; height, 5ft 10ins. Appears not to have sustained any injuries at Waterloo. Served 20 years with the Regiment. Discharged through Chelsea Pension office, April 1830, as unfit for service following an injury to his spine, sustained when he fell from his horse in 1829. His general conduct was described as very good indeed.

Private Peter GIBSON*
Born, Stoney Kirk, Wigton, Lanark; a labourer by trade. Enlisted, March 1801; height, 5ft 8ins. Appears not to have sustained any injuries at Waterloo. Served 18 years with the Regiment. Discharged through Chelsea Pension office, March 1818, due to general debility. His general conduct was described as good.

Private Alexander GOURLEY
Enlisted, January 1797; a weaver by trade. Enlistment height, 5ft 9ins. Appears not to have sustained any injuries at Waterloo. Discharged through Kilmainham Pension office, 1818, due to rheumatism.
   Waterloo Medal extant (Provenance: Glendining 1989).

Private John HAMILTON
Enlisted, April 1807. Appears not to have sustained any injuries at Waterloo.

Private James HART*

Born, Paisley, Renfrew; a blacksmith by trade. Enlistment height, 5ft 6ins. Appears not to have sustained any injuries at Waterloo. Attended the wounded horses at Brussels, July 1815. Served 24 years with the Regiment. Discharged through Chelsea Pension office, 1826, due to being worn out. His general conduct was described as very good.

Private William HICKLING

Enlisted, April 1813. Appears not to have sustained any injuries at Waterloo.

Private William HILL

Enlisted, 26th July 1793. At Waterloo wounded in the left leg by a lance and dislocated his right shoulder after falling from his horse which was killed.

Private Alexander HUNTER*

Born, Gorbals, Glasgow; a labourer by trade. Enlisted, 1812; height, 5ft 9ins. Appears not to have sustained any injuries at Waterloo. Sick in the Regimental Hospital, August 1815. Served 24 years with the Regiment. Discharged through Chelsea Pension office, 1835. His general conduct was described as very good.

Private Alexander INGRAM*

Born, Kilmarnock; a gunsmith by trade. Enlistment height, 5ft 9ins. Appears not to have sustained any injuries at Waterloo. Served 26 years with the Regiment. Discharged through Chelsea Pension office, July 1835, due to the effects of long service and inflammation of the lungs causing difficulty in breathing. His general conduct was described as tolerably good.

Private James LAPSLEY*

Born, Paisley, Renfrew; a weaver by trade. Enlisted, 1810; height, 5ft 10ins. Promoted Corporal. Appears not to have sustained any injuries at Waterloo. Served 27 years with the Regiment. Discharged through Chelsea Pension office, January 1836, because of poor memory due to inflammation of the brain. His general conduct was described as good.

Private Richard LEE

Enlisted, 22nd July 1813, age 18 years. Appears not to have sustained any injuries at Waterloo.

Private William LEVITT*

Born, St. Martins in the Field, London; a brass founderer by trade. Enlisted, 12th February 1812, Manchester, age 22 years; height, 5ft 11ins. Wounded at Waterloo in the right shoulder, the left wrist and the left foot and was sent to Brussels to recover. His general conduct was described as excellent, though he was demoted from Corporal, December 1815. Served 23 years with the Regiment. Discharged through Chelsea Pension office, 1835, due to debility contracted during service.

Married, three children, lived at 33 Fleming Road, Walworth, Newington, London. Died, August 1866, due to paraplegia; buried, Norwood cemetery, South London.

Waterloo Medal extant (Provenance: Allison collection).

Private George LONGWORTH

A labourer by trade. Served in the Princess Royals Fencible Cavalry, from 25th March 1799. Enlisted, November 1799; height, 5ft 7ins. Wounded at Waterloo by a lance in the forearm and by a shell in the leg. Served 22 years with the Regiment. Discharged through Kilmainham Pension office, November 1818, due to the effects of injuries sustained in combat, including lance wounds to the forearm, and leg wounds from a shell.

Private John M'KECHNY

Enlisted, October 1807. Appears not to have sustained any injuries at Waterloo.

Private David M'LELLAND*

Born, Beith, Glasgow; a labourer by trade. Enlisted, 1813; height, 5ft 8ins. Appears not to have sustained any injuries at Waterloo. Served 16 years with the Regiment. Discharged through Chelsea Pension office, 1827, due to palpitations and chronic rheumatism. His general conduct was described as good.

Private Hugh M'LELLAND*

Born, Mauchlin, Ayr; a weaver by trade. Enlisted, May 1805; height, 5ft 9ins. Appears not to have sustained any injuries at Waterloo. Then attended the wounded horses at Brussels. Sick in Regimental Hospital, August 1815. Served 24 years with the Regiment. Discharged through Chelsea Pension office, November 1827, due to being worn out. His general conduct was described as good.

Waterloo Medal extant (Provenance: Spink 1997).

Private James M'LINTOCK*

Born, Dumbarton; a shoemaker by trade. Initially served with Lanark Fencible Cavalry May 1799–May 1801. Enlisted, July 1804; height, 5ft 8in. Appears not to have sustained any injuries at Waterloo. Served 17 years. Discharged through Chelsea Pension office, 1818, due to general debility. His general conduct was described as good.

Private William MacKIE

Born, Falkirk; a shoemaker by trade. Appears not to have sustained any injuries at Waterloo. Transferred to No. 5 Troop, July 1815. He was one of the celebrated Falkirk 13.

Private John McARTHUR

Born, Barony, Glasgow; a labourer by trade. Killed in action at Waterloo.

Private Alexander M'LEOD*

Born, Fil Michael, Argyle; a shoemaker by trade. Enlisted, 1811; height, 5ft 8ins. Reported as sick in hospital, 1815. Served 24 years with the Regiment. Discharged through Chelsea Pension office, 1833, due to disability. He was described as a good efficient soldier

Private John MARTIN*

Born, Barony, Glasgow; a labourer by trade. Enlisted, January 1813, age 17 years. Served 24 years with the Regiment. Appears not to have sustained any injuries at Waterloo. Transferred to No. 4 Troop, July 1815. Sick in hospital, August 1815. Discharged through Chelsea Pension office, July 1835, being unfit due to inflammation of the lungs, contracted whilst on duty.

Waterloo Medal extant (Provenance: Dix Noonan Webb 2004).

Private James MASTERTON

Born, Falkirk, 1790, son of John Masterton, joiner, and Janet Marshall, his wife. Enlisted, Glasgow, 1810. At Waterloo, sustained a severe sabre wound and was carried from the battlefield and taken to Rouen where he convalesced for six weeks.

Eventually settled back in his native town, Falkirk; married twice, had a son and a daughter. In 1841, then age 50 years, he lived in East Burn Bridge (now East Bridge Street) and worked as a joiner. The 1851 census lists him as a widower at Silver Row, still a joiner. Died, May 1861. He was the last but one of the celebrated Falkirk 13 to die.

Private George MAUCHLIN

Born, Rutherglen, Lanark; a labourer by trade. Enlistment height, 5ft 10ins. Appears not to have sustained any injuries at Waterloo. Served 11 years with the Regiment. Discharged due to being unfit and having an incurable fistula. His general conduct was described as good.

Private William MERRIE

Born, 7th April 1798. Enlisted, 19th November 1813. Appears not to have sustained any injuries at Waterloo.

Private Robert MILLER

Born, 9th February 1796. His surname may have been Millar. Enlisted, February 1813. Appears not to have sustained any injuries at Waterloo. After Waterloo, transferred to No. 4 Troop. Probably a member of the celebrated Falkirk 13.

Private James PATERSON

Born, 10th April 1775, from Newlands; a tailor by trade. Enlisted, 25th May 1811. Appears not to have sustained any injuries at Waterloo. Attended the wounded horses after Waterloo.

Waterloo Medal extant (Provenance: Glendining 1990).

Private Robert PATERSON

Born, 12th August 1780. Enlisted, November 1797. Appears not to have sustained any injuries at Waterloo.

Waterloo Medal extant.

Private Hugh PATTISON

Enlisted, 21st August 1811, age 22 years. Appears not to have sustained any injuries at Waterloo.

Private Andrew PEDEN

Born, Avehinsleck, Ayr, Peden; a weaver by trade. Enlisted, February 1800; height, 5ft 9ins. Appears not to have sustained any injuries at Waterloo. Served 22 years with the Regiment. Discharged due to chronic rheumatism and being worn out.

Private John ROBERTSON

Born, Paisley; a weaver by trade. Killed in action at Waterloo.

Private Samuel SIFTON*

Born, Thornbury, Hereford; a labourer by trade. Enlisted, July 1805; height, 5ft 8ins. Appears not to have sustained any injuries at Waterloo. Served 24 years with the Regiment. Discharged through Chelsea Pension office, November 1827, due to being worn out from length of service. His general conduct was described as good

Waterloo Medal extant (Provenance: Dix Noonan Webb 2010).

Private James SMITH*

Born, Lymington, Ayr; a blacksmith by trade. Enlisted, 1813; height, 5ft 8ins. Appears not to have sustained any injuries at Waterloo. Served 12 years with the Regiment, Discharged through Chelsea Pension office, 1824, at Newcastle, because of impaired vision because of amaurosis (blindness due to a blockage of the blood supply to the retina). His general conduct was described as good.

Private William SMITH

Born, Ashbourne, Derbyshire; a blacksmith by trade. Enlistment height, 5ft 9ins. Appears not to have sustained any injuries at Waterloo. Served 19 years with the Regiment. Discharged spitting blood and ruptured due to over exertion in the riding school.

Private James STRUTHERS

Enlisted, January 1812. Appears not to have sustained any injuries at Waterloo.

Private Joseph TUCKY*

Born, Maidstone, Kent; a bricklayer by trade. Enlisted, 1804; height, 5ft 10ins. Appears not to have sustained any injuries at Waterloo. Served 15 years with the Regiment. Discharged through Chelsea

Pension office, 1818, due to a pectoral (chest) complaint caused by exposure to wet conditions. His general conduct was described as good.

Waterloo Medal extant (Provenance: Dix Noonan Webb 2005).

Private James WAITE*

Born, Iron Acton, Gloucester; a miner by trade. Enlisted, 1805; height, 5ft 8ins. Appears not to have sustained any injuries at Waterloo. Served 14 years with the Regiment. Discharged through Chelsea Pension office, 1818, due to enlarged varicose veins of the right arm from the exertion of riding. His general conduct was described as good.

Private James WALKER*

Born, Ratcliffe, Bury; a bleacher by trade. Enlisted, 1812; height, 5ft 8ins. Appears not to have sustained any injuries at Waterloo. Served 14 years with the Regiment. Discharged through Chelsea Pension office, 1824, due to a double rupture contracted in service. His general conduct was described as good.

Private Francis WELLS

Enlisted, 20th April, 1805, Nottingham. Appears not to have sustained any injuries at Waterloo.

Private William WILKERSON

Enlisted, 12th August 1805, Southampton. Appears not to have sustained any injuries at Waterloo.

Private George WILLET*

Born, Nantwich, Cheshire; a tailor by trade. Enlisted, 1811; height, 5ft 9ins. At Waterloo wounded by a lance wound in the loin and severe contusion due to falling from his horse which was killed. At Brussels recovering from wounds, July to September 1815. Served 29 years with the Regiment. Discharged through Chelsea Pension office, 1839, owing to disability due to length of service. His general conduct was described as extremely good.

Private Robert WILSON

Born, Gorbals, Glasgow; a weaver by trade. Enlisted from the Lanark Fencibles, 1799. Appears not to have sustained any injuries at Waterloo.

Private William WILSON

Enlisted, 3rd July, 1808, Glasgow. Appears not to have sustained any injuries at Waterloo. Promoted Corporal.

Private Archibald WRIGHT*

Born, Glasgow; a flesher by trade. Enlisted, 1810; height, 5ft 7ins. At Waterloo, received a lance wound in the right leg and musket shot in the back. At Brussels recovering from wounds, June to September 1815. Served 17 years with the Regiment. Discharged through Chelsea Pension office, 1825, due to consumption (tuberculosis) and wounds. His general conduct was described as very good.

Cheney's Troop

Captain Edward CHENEY

Eldest son of Robert Cheney, Meynell Langley, Derbyshire. Lieutenant, 1794; Captain, May 1800; Brevet Major, 1812; Major, July 1815. Joined De Watteville's Regiment on Half Pay 1818; Colonel, 1837.

Served with the Scots Greys in Flanders and at Waterloo, commanding the Regiment during the last three hours of the battle when he had five horses killed under him. Captain Cheney led the surviving remnants of the Regiment off the battlefield. Awarded a CB in 1816.

Married Elizabeth Ayre whose father lived at Gaddesby Hall. Colonel Cheney subsequently inherited the Estate. Died, Gaddesby, Leicestershire, 3 March 1847. Commemorated with an impressive white marble, life-size sculpture in Gaddesby church confirming the loss of five mounts. It depicts the death of one of his trusty mounts and has a scene from the battle carved in high relief on the front of the pedestal.

Lieutenant James GAPE

Born, St Albans, Herts, son of Reverend James Gape. Enlisted as Cornet without purchase, 1813, age 16; Lieutenant, by purchase, May 1815 (possibly the youngest Lieutenant in the Scots Greys at Waterloo.)

His 'Waterloo' saddle is in the Regimental Museum with evidence of musket ball holes, show how close he was to being seriously wounded. In a letter home, Gape describes riding with Lieutenant Colonel Inglis Hamilton before the latter lost control and charged to his death; he also confirms the deaths of General Ponsonby, Captain Reignolds, and Lieutenant Carruthers.

Waterloo Medal believed to be extant.

Lieutenant Francis STUPART

Son of John Stupart, Clackmannen. Joined Dundee, 4th Forfarshire Volunteer Infantry, June 1803. Cornet, Scots Greys, 5th May 1808; Lieutenant by purchase, 1809; Captain, July 1815 (in place of Cheney who obtained a Brevet Majority); Half Pay, 1816–1844. Wounded at Waterloo.

Married, Anne, daughter of John Jameson of Alloa, Dublin, 8th April 1821; three children. Died, 1860; buried, Warriston Cemetery, Edinburgh.

Waterloo Medal sent to 7 St Andrews Square, Glasgow; he is shown wearing it in his portrait.

Waterloo Medal extant, Regimental Museum

Troop Sergeant Major Alexander DINGWELL*

Born, Inveresk, Musselburgh; a labourer by trade. Enlisted, 1791; height, 5ft 11ins. Appears not to have sustained any injuries at Waterloo. Served 26 years with the Regiment. Discharged, 1816, due to being appointed Provost Sergeant, Edinburgh.

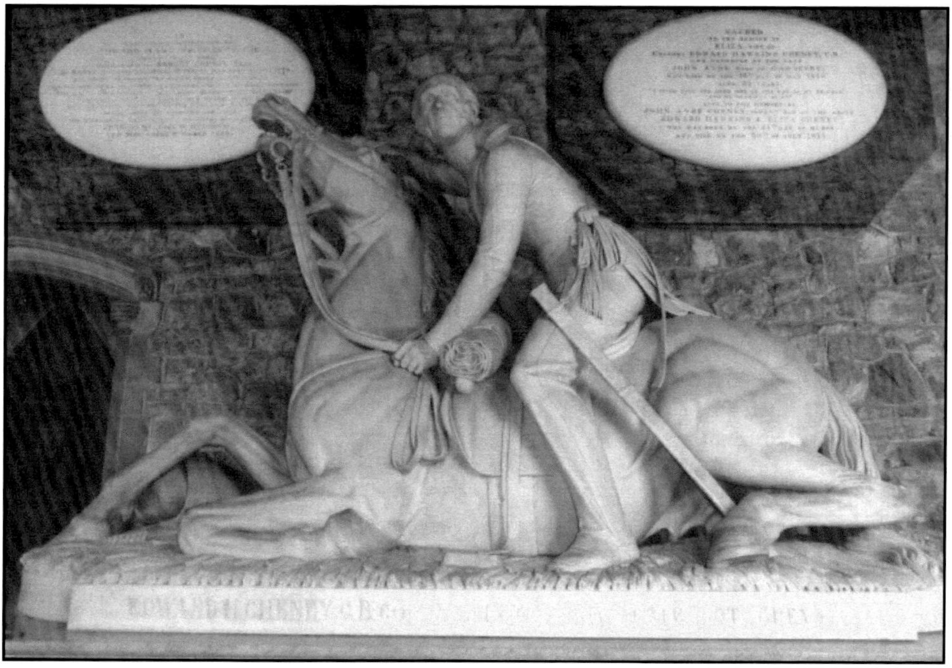

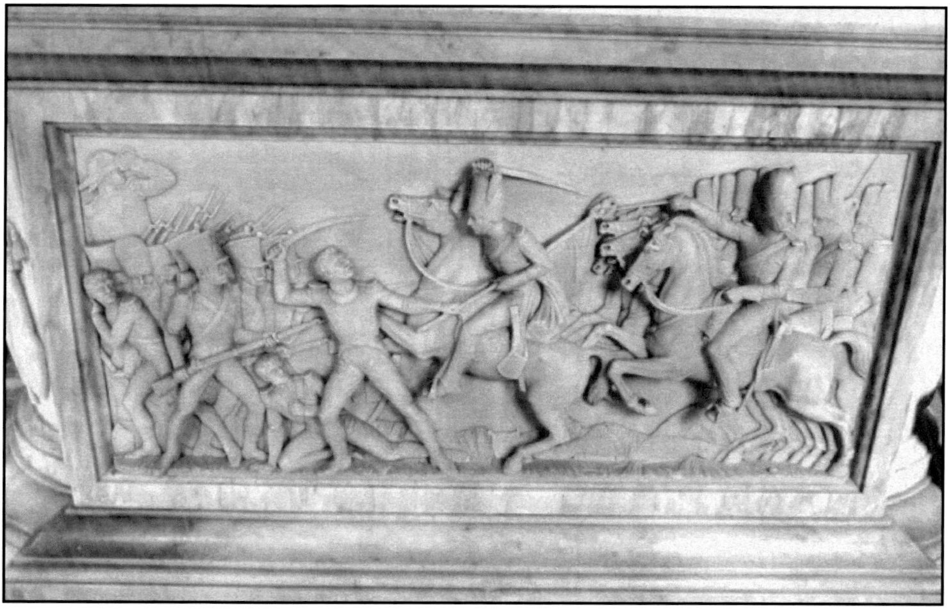

Above: Monument to Colonel Edward Cheney in St Luke's church, Gaddesby, Leicestershire
Below: Scene of Waterloo in high relief on the pedestal of the Cheney monument

Portraits of Lieutenant Francis Stupart and his wife Anne, together with a collection of swords belonging to the officer including a French sword, possibly acquired at Waterloo

Sergeant Donald CAMPBELL

Born, Latheron Wick, Caithness; a labourer by trade. Enlistment height, 5ft 10ins. Appears not to have sustained any injuries at Waterloo. Served 26 years with the Regiment; then in Rothesay Fencibles for two years. Discharged due to being worn out.

Sergeant William DICKIE

Enlisted, 16th April 1795. Appears not to have sustained any injuries at Waterloo.
Waterloo Medal extant, Robert Gottlieb collection.

Sergeant William HARVEY*

Born, Alfreton, Derby; a labourer by trade. Enlisted, March 1806; height, 5ft 9ins. Wounded at Waterloo. Served 24 years with the Regiment. Discharged through Chelsea Pension office, June 1828, due to being worn out. His general conduct was described as very good.
Waterloo Medal extant (Provenance: Glendining 1926).

Sergeant Alexander RENNIE*

Born, Whitburn, Glasgow; a labourer by trade. Enlisted, 1793; height, 5ft 9ins. Served in the campaigns of 1793, 1794 and 1795. Appears not to have sustained any injuries at Waterloo. Served 27 years with the Regiment. Discharged through Chelsea Pension office, 1818, due to a pectoral (chest) complaint and being worn out. His general conduct was described as extremely good and very useful in the Regiment.

Corporal Robert HAIR

Enlisted, April 1805, Nottingham. His surname may have been Hair. Wounded at Waterloo, sent to Brussels to recover.

Corporal William LAIRD

Born, Paisley, Renfrew; a weaver by trade. Enlisted, November 1808; height, 5ft 9ins. Suffered a severe wound to the right side of his back at Waterloo. Served eight years with the Regiment. Discharged through Chelsea Pension office, 1816, due to disability from a gunshot wound received in battle. His general conduct was described as excellent and that he was a clean soldier.

Corporal John LONG

Enlisted, March 1800. Wounded at Waterloo, sent to Brussels to recover. Discharged through Kilmainham Pension office.
Waterloo Medal extant (Provenance: Glendining 1990).

Corporal James ROSS*

Born, Drogheda; a gardener by trade. Enlisted, 1805; height, 5ft 9ins. Received a gunshot wound to the right arm at Waterloo. Sent to England, September 1815. Served 12 years with the Regiment. Discharged at Rouen through Chelsea Pension office, October 1815. His general conduct was described by Major Hankin: 'Corporal Ross has always been a real exemplary good soldier in every aspect, a very steady intelligent man, always alive and active for the good of the Regiment'.

Trumpeter John Henry SIBOLD

Born, Swartzberg, Saxony; a musician by trade. Enlistment height, 5ft 10ins. Appears not to have sustained any injuries at Waterloo. Served 19 years with the Regiment. Discharged, 1821, due to being unfit and prone to sore legs. His general conduct was described as good.

Waterloo Medal extant (Provenance: Buckland Dix & Wood 1994).

Private George ALISON

Born, Renfrew; a weaver by trade. Enlisted, July 1798; height, 5ft 7ins. Appears not to have sustained any injuries at Waterloo. Served 26 years with the Regiment. Discharged through Chelsea Pension office, due to imperfect vision of the right eye following an attack of ophthalmia. Admitted to pension, 25th September 1822, aged 45 years.

Private Matthew ANDERSON*

Born, Kilmarnock, Ayr; a weaver by trade. Enlisted, August 1812; height, 5ft 8ins. Appears not to have sustained any injuries at Waterloo. Served 24 years with the Regiment. Discharged through Chelsea Pension office, 1834, due to pulmonary affection (*sic*) and general debility. His general conduct was described as tolerably good.

Private Archibald BELL

Enlisted, May 1805. Appears not to have sustained any injuries at Waterloo.

Private Hugh BICKET*

Born, Paisley; a weaver by trade. Enlisted, May 1798; height, 5ft 8ins. Appears not to have sustained any injuries at Waterloo. Served 21 years with the Regiment. Discharged through Chelsea Pension office, 1818, due to being worn out and debility. His general conduct was described as extremely good.

Private John BRASH*

Born, Glasgow; a weaver by trade. Enlisted, August 1800; height, 5ft 10ins. Sustained two severe lance wounds in the back at Waterloo. Served 24 years with the Regiment. Discharged through Chelsea Pension office, 1823, due to being worn out and chronic rheumatism.

Private Charles BURGESS

Enlisted, January 1808. Wounded at Waterloo.

Private James BUTTON

Enlisted, August 1804. Wounded at Waterloo, sent to Brussels to recover. Discharged, 14th November 1815.

Private John CALDER
Enlisted, July 1813. Wounded at Waterloo, sent to Brussels to recover.

Private Samuel CLARKE
Enlisted, March 1804. Wounded at Waterloo, sent to Brussels to recover.

Private John COUPLAND
Born, Kirkmahoe, Dumfriesshire; a merchant by trade. Killed in action at Waterloo.

Private Archibald CRAIG
Enlisted, April 1812. Appears not to have sustained any injuries at Waterloo.

Private Robert CRAIG
Born, Rutherglen, Lanarkshire; a labourer by trade. Killed in action at Waterloo.

Private David CRIGHTON*
Born, Dalmington, Ayr; a labourer by trade. Enlisted, January 1810; height, 5ft 7ins. Sustained a gunshot wound of the belly whilst in action at Waterloo. His injuries were probably so severe that he was thought unlikely to survive, hence he appears erroneously on Almack's Roll of Honour. Served seven years with the Regiment. Discharged through Chelsea Pension office, October 1815, due to wounds. Died 1851.
  Waterloo Medal extant, private collection (Provenance: Sotheby 1986, EE Needes collection)

Private John CROMBIE*
Born, Stenten, Haddington; a labourer by trade. Lothian Fencible Cavalry, October 1795–March 1800. Enlisted, March 1800; height, 5ft 10ins. Appears not to have sustained any injuries at Waterloo. Served 29 years with the Regiment. Discharged, July 1823, due to being worn out and chronic rheumatism as a result of exposure to the cold. His general conduct was described as good.
  Waterloo Medal extant, Regimental Museum.

Private Thomas CROWE
Enlisted, October 1812, age 24 years. Appears not to have sustained any injuries at Waterloo.

Private Major DICKINSON
Enlisted, February 1807. Appears to have not sustained any injuries at Waterloo.

Private Peter DRYSDALE
Enlisted, April 1812. Appears not to have sustained any injuries at Waterloo.

The pitting on the obverse of Private David Crighton's Waterloo Medal 1815
indicates it was worn over a considerable period of time

Edge of Crighton's medal illustrating the classic impressed naming on the Waterloo Medal 1815

Private John FRASER

Born, Paisley; a weaver by trade. Appears not to have sustained any injuries at Waterloo. Following Waterloo, he is described as attending a wounded officer.

Private George GRAY

Enlisted, December 1809. Appears not to have sustained any injuries at Waterloo.
  Waterloo Medal extant (Provenance: EE Needes collection 1925).

Private William GUNN

Enlisted, August 1812. Appears not to have sustained any injuries at Waterloo.
  Waterloo Medal extant (Provenance: Glendining 1935).

Private James HAMILTON Senior*

Born, Paisley, Glasgow; a wright by trade. Enlisted, 1804; height, 5ft 10ins. Appears not to have sustained any injuries at Waterloo. Served 24 years with the Regiment. Discharged through Chelsea Pension office, 1827, due to being worn out. His general conduct was described as good.

Private James HAMILTON Junior

Born, Barony; a painter by trade. Appears not to have sustained any injuries at Waterloo.

Private Robert HAMILTON

Born, Kilmarnock; a farmer by trade. Died of wounds sustained at Waterloo, 19th June 1815.

Private Allan HARVIE

Born, Hayfield, Derbyshire; a weaver by trade. Died of wounds sustained at Waterloo, 18th July 1815.

Private David HENDERSON

Enlisted, July 1797. Wounded at Waterloo; sent to Brussels to recover.

Private Adam HEPBURN

Enlisted, August 1807. Appears not to have sustained any injuries at Waterloo.

Private William HUBBARD

Enlisted, January 1806. Appears not to have sustained any injuries at Waterloo.

Private Thomas JOHNSTON

Enlisted, May 1812. Wounded at Waterloo, sent to Brussels to recover.

Private John JUDD*

Born, Farringdon, Berks; a shoemaker by trade. Enlisted, 1800; height, 5ft 7ins. Wounded at Waterloo. Served 19 years with the Regiment. Discharged through Chelsea Pension office, due to being worn out and having a severe back injury as the result of falling from his horse when it was shot at Waterloo. His general conduct was described as very good.

Private William LOCKEAD (LOCHEAD)

Enlisted, December 1796. His surname may have been Lochead. Severely wounded at Waterloo, sent to Brussels to recover.

Waterloo Medal extant (Provenance: Glendining 1992, Jubilee collection).

Private Andrew M'CLURE*

Born, Kilmarnock, Ayr; a weaver by trade. Enlisted, 1805; height, 5ft 8ins. Appears not to have sustained any injuries at Waterloo. Served 14 years with the Regiment. Discharged through Chelsea Pension office, 1818, due to asthma and a diseased spleen contracted in service. His general conduct was described as very good.

Private Archibald M'FARLAN*

Born, Paisley, Renfrew; a collier by trade. Enlisted, 1813; height, 5ft 9ins. Appears not to have sustained any injuries at Waterloo. Served ten years with the Regiment. Discharged through Chelsea Pension office, 1821, due to chest problems tending towards consumption. His general conduct was very good.

Private John M'INTYRE*

Born, Barony, Glasgow; a gardener by trade,. Enlisted, 1811; height, 5ft 9ins. Appears not to have sustained any injuries at Waterloo. Served 19 years with the Regiment. Discharged through Chelsea Pension office, 1828, due to delirium tremens. His general conduct was described as good.

Private Andrew M'KENDRICK*

Born, Glasgow; a tinsmith by trade. Enlisted, 25th September 1807; height, 5ft 9ins. Right hand shattered by grape shot, and two musket balls to his right thigh, both at Waterloo. Served ten years with the Regiment. Discharged through Chelsea Pension office, February 1816, due to his wounds. He was described as a gallant soldier severely wounded.

Waterloo Medal extant, author's collection (Provenance: Glendining 1957, ex-Ernie Bell collection).

Private William M'KINLEY*

Born, Wigton, Galloway; a labourer by trade. Enlisted, 1805; height, 5ft 10ins. Appears not to have sustained any injuries at Waterloo. Served 15 years with the Regiment. Discharged through Chelsea pension office, 1818, due to a shoulder injury resulting from a horse falling on him, May 1817. His general conduct was described as extremely good.

Waterloo Medal extant (Provenance: Dix Noonan Webb).

Private Alexander M'PHERSON*

Born, Falkirk, Stirling; a weaver by trade. Enlisted, 1806; height, 5ft 8ins. Served 19 years with the Regiment. Severely wounded at Waterloo. Discharged through Chelsea pension office, 1823, due to his term of service having expired. His general conduct was described as very good. A member of the celebrated Falkirk 13.

Private Robert MAKIN

Born, Inksworth, Bedford; a labourer by trade. Enlistment height, 5ft 10ins. Wounded in the right side at Waterloo. Served 13 years with the Regiment. Served with 7 Veteran Battalion until 1821.

Private James MANN*

Born, Mearns, Renfrew; a wright by trade. Enlisted, 1805; height, 5ft 8ins. Appears not to have sustained any injuries at Waterloo. Served 24 years with the Regiment. Discharged through Chelsea Pension office, 1828, due to being worn out. His general conduct was described as very good.

Private Gavin MATHER

Born, Hamilton; a weaver by trade. Killed in action at Waterloo

Private William MATHIE*

Born, Neilston, Renfrew; a labourer by trade. Enlisted, 1813; height, 5ft 11ins. Appears not to have sustained any injuries at Waterloo. Served 15 years with the Regiment. Discharged through Chelsea Pension office, 1827, due to being because of a diseased scalp. His general conduct was described as good.

Private Robert MUIRHEAD

Born, Glasgow; a flesher by trade. Killed in action at Waterloo.

Private Peter MURRAY

Born, Tippermuir, Perth; a labourer by trade. Killed in action at Waterloo.

Private Thomas OMAN

Enlisted, July 1812, age 24 years. Appears not to have sustained any injuries at Waterloo. At Brussels sick July, 1815.

Waterloo Medal extant (Provenance: Spink 1878).

Private David RAMPTON

Born, Overton, Ayrshire; a labourer by trade. Enlistment height, 5ft 10ins. Wounded several times at Waterloo, including a sabre cut to the face, musket shot in the left thigh, two lance wounds in the right side, and similar wounds on the left. Served 16 years with the Regiment. Discharged through Kilmainham Pension office, May 1821, due to chronic rheumatism.

Waterloo Medal extant (Provenance: Glendining 1903).

Private Thomas ROBERTSON
Born, Neilston; a weaver by trade. Killed in action at Waterloo

Private James RONALD
Enlisted, January 1811. Wounded at Waterloo, sent to Brussels to recover.

Private James ROSE
Born, Glasgow; a weaver by trade. Killed in action at Waterloo

Private Andrew SCOTT*
Born, Lanark; a weaver by trade. Enlisted, 18th March 1814; height, 5ft 10 ins. Appears not to have sustained any injuries at Waterloo. Served 24 years with the Regiment. Discharged through Chelsea Pension office, 1838, due to chronic rheumatism. His general conduct was described as good.

Private James SCOTT*
Born, High Church, Glasgow; a mason by trade. Enlisted, May 1813; height, 5ft 8ins. Appears not to have sustained any injuries at Waterloo. Lost the use of his right arm as a consequence of a horse falling on him, whilst escorting the mail in Holland, 1821. Served ten years with the Regiment. Discharged through Chelsea Pension office, 1821. His general conduct was described as good.

Private John SPRAIKE (SPRACKE)
Born, 21st January 1783. Surname may have been Spracke. Enlisted, 23rd July 1800. Appears not to have sustained any injuries at Waterloo. Discharged through Kilmainham Pension office.

Private John STIRLING*
Born, Cathcart, Renfrew; a labourer by trade. Enlisted, March 1810; height, 5ft 10ins. Served 17 years with the Regiment. Wounded at Waterloo. Discharged through Chelsea Pension office, October 1823, due to being unfit as affected with phthisis (TB) and disease of the spleen and heart. His general conduct was described as very indifferent.

Private Robert STIRLING*
Born, Barony, Glasgow; a labourer by trade. Enlisted, November 1808; height, 5ft 8ins. Appears not to have sustained any injuries at Waterloo. Served 15 years with the Regiment. Discharged through Chelsea Pension office, following an accident when he injured his left testicle during a fall from his horse in Phoenix Park, Dublin, 1820. His general conduct was described as pretty good.

Private William STIRLING*
Born, Kilmarnock; a blacksmith by trade. Served Ayrshire Fencible Cavalry, August 1795–March 1800. Enlisted, 24th March 1800; height, 5ft 7ins. Appears not to have sustained any injuries at Waterloo. Served 28 years. Discharged through Chelsea Pension office, 23rd October 1820, due to being worn out with chronic rheumatism His general conduct was described as very good.

Private Thomas STOBO

Born, Abbey, Paisley; a weaver by trade. Enlistment height, 5ft 9ins. At 43, the oldest man to charge with the Scots Greys at Waterloo, where he was wounded. Served 24 years with the Regiment. Discharged due to chronic rheumatism. Died, 1852

Private Robert TAYLOR

Born, Barony, Glasgow; a weaver by trade. Killed in action at Waterloo.

Private Robert TEMPLE

Enlisted, June 1808. Appears not to have sustained any injuries at Waterloo.
   Waterloo Medal extant (Provenance: Hyde Greg collection 1887).

Private James THOMPSON

Born, New Mills, Ayr; a tailor by trade. Enlistment height, 5ft 8ins. Served 25 years with the Regiment. Appears not to have sustained any injuries at Waterloo. After Waterloo transferred to No. 5 Troop.

Private Thomas TIMPERLY

Born, 19th December 1788. Enlisted, 29th July 1805. Wounded at Waterloo, sent to Brussels to recover.

Private John TOMAN

Enlisted, November, 1814, age 18 years. After Waterloo, reported sick at Brussels.

Private John URIE

Born, Gorbals, Glasgow; a weaver by trade. Killed in action at Waterloo.

Private John WALLACE

Born, Kilmarnock; a labourer by trade. Appears not to have sustained any injuries at Waterloo.

Private William WATT*

Born, Inveresk, MidLothian; a blacksmith by trade. Enlisted, May 1805; height, 5ft 11ins. Appears not to have sustained any injuries at Waterloo. Served 18 years with the Regiment. Discharged, 1821, unfit for further service due to chronic rheumatism. His general conduct was described as good.
   Waterloo Medal extant (Provenance: Spink 1997).

Poole's Troop

Captain James POOLE

Lieutenant, 1797; Captain, May 1803; Brevet Major, June 1813; Brevet Lieutenant Colonel. Wounded at Waterloo and subsequently taken prisoner. Left the service due to mental ill health (possibly post-traumatic stress), 1817.

A letter from Captain Cheney to his wife, Elizabeth, dated 20th June 1815, confirms that Poole was wounded five times and taken prisoner. He describes the wounds as not being of 'material consequence'.

Lieutenant James WEMYSS

Cornet, August 1810; Lieutenant, September 1814; Captain, 1816; Major, 1826; Half Pay, 1827. Commanded his troop in the last charge of the regiment at Waterloo. Severely wounded in the arm.

Appointed High Constable of Durham. Died, October 1847.

Troop Sergeant Major James RUSSELL

Born, Barony, Glasgow; a mason by trade. Enlisted, 1798; height, 5ft 11ins. Fortunate to escape injury at Waterloo, unlike his horse which was severely wounded. During the action, he lost his entire kit which contained his valuable, much read bible, a possession which he later stated he missed the most. It was Russell's letter to his wife, one week after the battle, that was mainly responsible for the news of the great victory reaching Glasgow.

Served 25 years with the Regiment. Discharged, 1821, due to a severe contusion to his breast and right testicle during a riding accident. His general conduct was described as extremely good, an excellent soldier and a worthy man. After discharge, a steam boat harbour master (Broomielaw) on the banks of the Clyde. Died, Rutherglen, age 82.

Waterloo Medal extant (Provenance: Buckland Dix & Wood 1994).

Sergeant John BISHOP

Born, Hamilton, Lanark; a weaver by trade. Enlistment height, 5ft 8ins. Served 26 years with the Regiment. His general conduct was described as very good; Lieutenant Colonel Clarke stated that he displayed great gallantry at Waterloo.

Sergeant Archibald JOHNSTON

Born, Tinwall Loch Maben, Dumfries; a labourer by trade. Appears not to have sustained any injuries at Waterloo. Served 20 years, including over five years as a Troop Sergeant Major. Discharged due to being worn out.

Sergeant George RENNIE

Born, Glasgow; a weaver by trade. Died of wounds sustained at Waterloo, 25th June 1815.

Sergeant Thomas STODDART

Born, Newbottle, Edinburgh; a labourer by trade. Enlistment height, 5ft 8 ins. Wounded by a sabre cut to the forehead, impairing his sight; also wounds to left hand and fingers. Sent to England, 8th July. Served 15 years.

Corporal John CRAIG

Born, Barony; a labourer by trade. Killed in action at Waterloo.

Corporal Alexander GARDINER*

Born, New Kilpatrick, Dunbarton, 1794. Enlisted, January 1809. Troop Sergeant Major, 1826. Wounded at Waterloo. Served 26 years with the Regiment, including eight as Sergeant. Discharged, 1835, Dalkeith, age 41 years.

Died, 1848, probably at Oswestry where he was thought to reside. His son served in the Crimea with the Scots Greys and was rescued by Private Ramage who won the Victoria Cross for the action.

Waterloo Medal extant (Provenance: Dix Noonan Webb 2005, sold with family group).

Corporal James NELSON (NEILSON)

Born, 10th January 1788, His surname may have been Neilson. Enlisted, 17th June 1805. Appears not to have sustained any injuries at Waterloo.

Corporal John WALLACE

Born, Kilmarnock, Ayr; a labourer by trade. Enlistment height, 5ft 10ins. Sustained a sabre wound to the right arm at Waterloo. Served 19 years with the Regiment, including five months as Corporal and 18 months as Sergeant. Discharged, 1817. His general conduct described was extremely good and it was stated that he displayed great gallantry at Waterloo.

Trumpeter Peter BUNCLE

Born, Faversham, Kent; a labourer by trade. Enlistment height, 5ft 9ins. Trumpeter at Waterloo; Corporal, 1820. Appears not to have sustained any injuries at Waterloo. Served 30 years with the Regiment, including seven as Sergeant. Discharged due to being worn out and incontinent of urine.

Waterloo Medal extent (Provenance: Spink 2005).

Private John ALEXANDER

Enlisted, August 1806. Appears not to have sustained any injuries at Waterloo. After the battle was at Brussels attending the wounded horses.

Waterloo Medal extant (Provenance: Allison collection).

Private John BROOKES

Born, Heaton Norris, near Stockport; a farmer by trade. Killed in action at Waterloo.

Private Thomas BROWN

Born, Monkland; a shoemaker by trade. Killed in action at Waterloo.

Private James BRUCE

Born, Bathgate, Linlithgow; a baker by trade. Enlisted, 1812; height, 5ft 10ins approx. Sustained sabre cut to left elbow at Waterloo. Served five years with the Regiment. Invalided, 8th September 1815. His general conduct was recorded as having been carried out in an exemplary manner.

Waterloo Medal extant (Provenance: Liverpool Medal Company 1984).

Private William CHRISTIE

Born, Auchterarder; a labourer by trade. Killed in action at Waterloo.

Private David CRAIG

Enlisted, April 1813. Appears not to have sustained any injuries at Waterloo.

Waterloo Medal extant (Provenance: Spink 1949).

Private James CRAWFORD

Born, High Church, Glasgow. Enlisted, November 1809. Appears not to have sustained any injuries at Waterloo. Served 22 years with the Regiment. His general conduct was described as very good.

Private Joseph CROWE (CROW)

Enlisted, October 1812, age 20 years. His surname sometimes appears as Crow. Appears not to have sustained any injuries at Waterloo.

Private Thomas DAWSON

Born, Ambleside; a labourer by trade. Killed in action at Waterloo.

Private John DODDS

Born, Berwick on Tweed; a sadler by trade. Killed in action at Waterloo.

Private Alexander DONALDSON

Born, Kinclaven, Perth; a mason by trade. Enlistment height, 5ft 8ins. Severely wounded at Waterloo by gunshot in the back, breast and both thighs; lance wounds to right breast and left thigh. Served 21 years with th Regiment. He was described as a gallant soldier, clean and active.

Private William ERSKINE

Enlisted, March 1811. Appears not to have sustained any injuries at Waterloo.

Private James FERGUSON

Born, Barony; a weaver by trade. Killed in action at Waterloo.

Private John FROST

Born, Tutbury; a labourer by trade. Killed in action at Waterloo.

Private Gavin GIBSON

Born, Beith, Ayr; a baker by trade. Enlisted, June 1811; height, 5ft 9 ins. Appears not to have sustained any injuries at Waterloo. Served seven years with the Regiment. Discharged, 1818, due to ruptures because of over exertion. His general conduct was described as good.

Private Robert GILCHRIST

Born, Kilmarnock; resided, Paisley; a weaver by trade. Enlisted, August 1806. A severe injury to his abdomen at Quatre Bras and a slight wound to his face at Waterloo. Served ten years with the Regiment. Discharged, August 1816, on a pension, 6d per day, upgraded in 1859 to 9d.

Private Thomas GOODS

Born, Panckern, Hereford; a labourer by trade. Enlisted, March 1804; height, 5ft 9ins. Appears not to have sustained any injuries at Waterloo. Served 22 years with the Regiment. Discharged, 1826, due to being worn out. His general conduct was described as very good.

Waterloo Medal extant (Provenance: Sotheby 1928, Colonel Murray collection).

Private Gavin JOHNSTON

Born, Old Monkland; a labourer by trade. Killed in action at Waterloo.

Private James KENNEDY

Born, Dumfries; a labourer by trade. Enlisted, February 1814; height, 5ft 10ins. Wounded at Waterloo. Served two years. Discharged due to lance wounds to the body and a contusion of the side sustained at Waterloo. He was described as a clean good soldier.

Waterloo Medal extant (Provenance: Dix Noonan Webb).

Private Alexander LANDER

Born, Lauder, Edinburgh; a tailor by trade. Enlisted, February 1798; height, 5ft 9ins. Appears not to have sustained any injuries at Waterloo. Served 23 years with the Regiment. Discharged, 1821, due to being unfit for further service because of a double hernia. His general conduct was described as extremely good.

Private Robert LAWRIE (LOURIE/LOWRIE)

Enlisted, June 1809. His surname also appears as Lourie and Lowrie. Severely wounded at Waterloo and found lying on the ground suffering from the effect of 18 sabre wounds from which he was fortunate to survive; sent to England to recover. His father died whilst he was in Belgium and Lawrie inherited 12,000 pounds.

Private William LEACH

Born, Northwich, Cheshire; a cotton spinner by trade. Killed in action at Waterloo.

Private Andrew LEES

Enlisted, November 1808. Appears not to have sustained any injuries at Waterloo.

Private William LOCH (LOCK/LOCKS)

Enlisted, December 1812. His surname also spelt Lock(s). Wounded at Waterloo and sent to Brussels. Lieutenant Colonel Charles Wyndham reported that Lock was severely wounded, sustaining 18 lance wounds, but survived the ordeal.

Private Fred M'VICAR

Born, Rutherglen, Lanark; a weaver by trade. Enlisted, March 1793; height, 5ft 10ins. Served in the Napoleonic campaigns of 1793, 1794, 1795. Left eye destroyed and severe wounds to the head received at Waterloo. Sent to England, 8th July 1815. Served 22 years with the Regiment. Discharged due to being blind in left eye. His general conduct was described as good.

Private George McALLA

Born, Carnwath; a carpenter by trade. Killed in action at Waterloo.

Private Hugh McAULEY

Born, Paisley; a labourer by trade. Killed in action at Waterloo.

Private David McGOWAN

Enlisted, January 1813. Sent to England because of wounds sustained at Waterloo. Received the Long Service and Good Conduct Medal (see page 18).

Private Robert McINDOE

Born, Govan, Glasgow; a weaver by trade. Enlisted, March 1800. Died of wounds sustained at Waterloo, 7th July 1815.

Private John McLAUCHLAN

Born, Dumfries; a labourer by trade. Killed in action at Waterloo.

Private Angus McPHERSON

Born, Moidart; a labourer by trade. Killed in action at Waterloo.

Private John MILLER

Enlisted, August 1795. Appears not to have sustained any injuries at Waterloo. Probably a member of the celebrated Falkirk 13.

Private William MITCHELL

Born, Kilmarnock; a hatter by trade. Killed in action at Waterloo.

Private Andrew MUIR

Enlisted, June 1806. Appears not to have sustained any injuries at Waterloo.
Waterloo Medal extant.

Private John NIELSON (NEILSON)

Enlisted, January 1807, Edinburgh. Surname also spelt Neilson. In Brussels wounded, 24th June 1815.

Private Edward NOAKS (NOAKES)

Enlisted, 25th November 1805, Birmingham. Appears not to have sustained any injuries at Waterloo.

Private Henry PALMER

Enlisted, June 1806. Reported sick in Regimental Hospital after Waterloo, but the nature of his illness or injury is unknown.
Waterloo Medal extant (Provenance: Dowell of Edinburgh 1926).

Private Thomas PHILIPS

Born, 15th July 1775, Selkirk, Roxborough. Enlisted, 25th February 1793; a weaver by trade. Wounded in the left shoulder by a musket ball at Waterloo and sent to Brussels. Served 22 years with the Regiment. Discharged, February 1816. He was described as an excellent and gallant soldier.

Private James RATCLIFF (RATTCLIFF)

Enlisted, June 1812, age 20 years. His surname also spelt Rattcliff. Appears not to have sustained injuries at Waterloo.

Private James RICHARDSON

Born, Stichell, Berwick; a labourer by trade. Enlistment height, 5ft 9ins. Appears not to have sustained any injuries at Waterloo. Served 22 years with the Regiment. Discharged due to being worn out.

Private Thomas ROBERTSON

Born, Neilston; a blacksmith by trade. Enlisted, September 1805. Appears not to have sustained any injuries at Waterloo.
Waterloo Medal extant, Regimental Museum.

Private William ROBERTSON

Born, Stewarton; a weaver by trade. Appears not to have sustained any injuries at Waterloo.

Private John ROWAT (ROWATT)

Born, 1st August 1788. Enlisted, 27th December 1805. Surname also spelt Rowatt. Appears not to have sustained any injuries at Waterloo.

Private John SALMON

Enlisted, June 1798. Reported sick in Regimental Hospital, August 1815, the nature of his illness or injury is unknown.

Private Matthew SCOTT

Born, Maybole, Ayr; a labourer by trade. Enlisted, August 1809; height, 6ft. Served 14 years with the Regiment. Discharged, 1824, due to sore legs and oedema partly resulting from falling off his horse at Waterloo. His general conduct was described as good.

Private Robert SMELLIE

Born, 1787, Old Monkland, Glasgow; a weaver by trade. Enlisted, June 1804; height, 5ft 7ins. Appears not to have sustained any injuries at Waterloo. Lost the first finger of right hand after being kicked by a horse. Served 12 years with the Regiment. Discharged, October 1816. He was described as a steady good soldier. Died, August 1862.

Waterloo Medal extant (Provenance: Dix Noonan Webb 1993).

Private James SMITH

Born, Kilmarnock; a shoemaker by trade. Killed in action at Waterloo.

Private Robert STEVENSON

Born, Kilmarnock; a weaver by trade. Enlisted, September 1793; height, 5ft 9ins. Appears not to have sustained any injuries at Waterloo. Served 22 years with the Regiment. Discharged, October 1817, due to being worn out by infirmity of service and chronic rheumatism. His general conduct was described as extremely good.

Private Adam TAIT

Born, 12th August 1780. Enlisted, 29th May 1798. Appears not to have sustained any injuries at Waterloo.

Private John THOMPSON

Born, Blantyre, Lanark; a weaver by trade. Enlisted, March 1810; height, 5ft 10ins. Sergeant, 1826. Appears not to have sustained any injuries at Waterloo. Served 22 years with the Regiment. Discharged, 1832. His general conduct was described as extremely good.

Private James TOVIE*

Born, Worcester; a labourer by trade. Enlisted, February 1794; height, 5ft 7ins. Appears not to have sustained any injuries at Waterloo. Served 22 years with the Regiment. Discharged, October 1816, due to a fracture of the right leg after falling from his horse whilst on duty. He was described as a worthy good man.

Private John WARK

Enlisted, December 1811. After Waterloo, sent to Brussels wounded and then to England.

Private Andrew WHITE*

Born, Nelson, Renfrew; a shoemaker by trade. Enlisted, March 1808; height, 5ft 8ins. Received severe wounds to the head and lesser wounds to the body at Waterloo. Served six years with the Regiment.

Private John WHITTON

Born, Packington; a labourer by trade. Killed in action at Waterloo.

Private William WILLIS*

Born, Pershore, Worcs; a labourer by trade. Enlisted, June 1798; height, 5ft 10ins. Appears not to have sustained any injuries at Waterloo. Served 22 years with the Regiment. Discharged, 1823, due to being worn out. His general conduct was described as good.

Private Robert WILSON*

Born, Stewarton, Ayr; a mason by trade. Enlisted, July 1804; height, 6ft 2ins. Appears not to have sustained any injuries at Waterloo. Served 18 years with the Regiment. Discharged due to being worn out and having a diseased spermatic cord. His general conduct was described as good.

Private William WRIGHT*

Born, Backway, Herts; a labourer by trade. Enlisted, October 1805; height, 5ft 8ins. Appears not to have sustained any injuries at Waterloo. Served 22 years with the Regiment. Discharged, 1827, due to being worn out. His general conduct was described as good.

Private Andrew WYLIE

Born, Stewarton; a flesher by trade. Killed in action at Waterloo.

Private Alexander YOUNG

Enlisted, May 1810. Appears not to have sustained any injuries at Waterloo.
   Waterloo Medal extant (Provenance: Sotheby 1995).

Private Nathaniel YOUNG

Enlisted, 17 June 1805. Appears not to have sustained any injuries at Waterloo.

Vernor's Troop

Captain Robert VERNOR

Lieutenant, September 1797; Captain, November 1804; Brevet Major, June 1814. Wounded at Waterloo. Major Vernor is believed to have rescued Lieutenant Colonel Hamilton's sword from the Waterloo battlefield. Retired after 30 years service, 1817, and then resided in Musselburgh. Died, 10th August 1827, age 64; buried, Inveresk churchyard, Scotland.

Lieutenant John MILLS

Cornet, December 1806; Lieutenant, May 1808; Captain, 19 July 1815; Brevet Major, 1822; Lieutenant Colonel 1826. Wounded at Waterloo. Died, 17th October 1837, age 53.

Waterloo Medal extant, Regimental Museum.

Cornet Francis Charlton KINCHANT

Born, Easton, Herefordshire. Son of Reverend Francis Kinchant. Cornet, January 1815. Keen to improve his equestrian skills, he wrote in one of his letters home: '... my improvement will enable me to share the honours my comrades are likely to reap'. In another letter to his friend, Mr Hall, he comments further on his horsemanship when he says he performs 'the drill daily with a brother officer who is junior to himself' (almost certainly Lemuel Shuldham). Kinchant charged with Sergeant Ewart at Waterloo and was later killed in that action, age 20. An account of his death is given in more detail later (see entry for Ewart, page 88). A memorial tablet, erected by his sister, is to be found in the parish church, Middleton on the Hill, Hereford, Worcestershire.

The actual troop in which this young officer served has not been confirmed. The balance of probability suggests it was Troop 5 as he was closely attached to Sergeant Charles Ewart. It is on this basis that his name is included here.

Waterloo Medal extant (Provenance: Robert Gottlieb collection).

Troop Sergeant Major William MacMILLAN

A painter by trade. Enlistment height, 5ft 7ins. Sustained lance wounds in his head and left wrist at Waterloo. Discharged through Kilmainham Pension office, 1818, due to rheumatism and deafness contracted in service.

Sergeant William CLARKE*

From Prestonpans, Haddington. Enlisted, 19th July 1803. Served four years as Private; five years as Corporal; eight years as Sergeant; six years as Sergeant Major.

Appears not to have sustained any injuries at Waterloo. Served 24 years with the Regiment. Discharged through Chelsea Pension office, 31st December 1825, due to being worn out from length of service. His conduct was described as good, except he had become involved in pecuniary difficulties.

Waterloo Medal extant (Provenance: Glendining 1903).

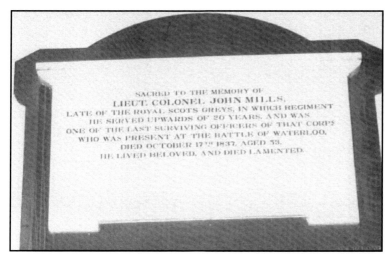

The Memorial Plaque to John Mills on the wall above the north porch in the church, Trull. Somerset

The Memorial Plaque to Francis Kinchant. The inscription reads:
Sacred to the Memory of Francis Charlton Kinchant Cornet in The Scots Greys
Only son of The Reverend F. Kinchant and Mary, his wife of Easton in this Parish.

This young man had only joined his Regiment long enough to gain the good opinion and regard of his brother Officers and his men, and to give great promise of becoming an ornament to the profession, when he was cut off at the Battle of Waterloo the 18th June 1815 in the 21st year of his age. Before he fell he gave decisive proof of the greatest zeal, humanity and courage. His sister, who erects this small memorial of her regret and love, endeavours to console herself by remembering that his career tho' short was honourable to himself and useful to his country.

Cornet Francis Charlton Kinchant's Waterloo Medal
With the kind permission of Mr Robert Gottlieb, from his Waterloo Collection

Sergeant Charles EWART

Born, Biddies Farm, near Elvanfoot, Kilmarnock, 1769. Enlisted, age 20. He was described as a giant of a man, his height being estimated conservatively at 6ft 4ins. In addition to his physical attributes he was an excellent horseman and an accomplished swordsman. These qualities he put to good use against the French, as he became a hero at Waterloo when he captured the eagle of the 45th French Regiment His account of the fight for the eagle differs somewhat from that of Dickson who, perhaps, is more pragmatic and less modest. Ewart records:

'I wrestled with my left hand for the coveted symbol. The Frenchman thrust at my groin but with the sword in my right hand I was able to parry the blow. I then cut him down with a slash that nearly severed his head. A Polish lancer then attacked, hurling his lance. The lance was brushed aside and with an upward stroke I cleft his head. A foot soldier fired his musket and rushed at me with his bayonet. It took little effort to dispose of this adversary'.

Ewart was also present at the tragic death of Cornet Francis Kinchant and avenged his death by slaying a treacherous French Officer whose life Ewart had spared earlier (at the request of Kinchant).

After Waterloo, promoted Ensign, 5th Veteran Battalion. Retired, 1821, pension 100 pounds per year. Died, 23rd March 1846, Davyhulme, Manchester, age 77 years, due to 'disease of the bladder'; buried, New Jerusalem Church, Bolton Street, Salford. In 1936, his remains were exhumed and reburied in Edinburgh. Death certificate, describes him as a Gentleman. (See: Portrait of Ewart, page 32; Ewart's death certificate, page 34)

Waterloo Medal and sword (used in capture of the French Eagle) extant, National War Museum Scotland.

Sergeant James STRUDWICK

Born, Ryegate (probably Reigate), Surrey; a tanner by trade. Killed in action at Waterloo.

Sergeant John TANNOCK

Born, Kilmarnock, Ayr; a weaver by trade. Enlisted, 1793; height, 5ft 9ins. Appears not to have sustained any injuries at Waterloo. Served 25 years with the Regiment. Discharged through Chelsea Pension office due to chronic rheumatism contracted in service. He was described as being of good character.

Waterloo Medal extant (Provenance: Christie 1965).

Corporal John DICKSON*

Born, Paisley, Renfrew, 1789; a weaver by trade. Enlisted, 1807, Glasgow. Underage Private, March–April 1807; Private, April 1807–April 1815; Corporal, April–October 1815; Sergeant, October 1815–July 1834. With the Scots Greys at Waterloo, he describes the Regiment's action in graphic detail (Low, 1911) and Sergeant Ewart's capture of the eagle of the 45th French Regiment. Dickson and his comrade Armour (probably James Armour of Fenton's Troop) encountered some open space, partly covered with bushes. There they found Ewart, surrounded by 5-6 French Infantrymen, trying to escape with one of their 'standards' (ie the Eagle). Dickson and his fellow Grey charged to their Sergeant's rescue. Already Ewart had disposed of two of the enemy and was about to strike a third who held the Eagle when he came in danger of being bayoneted himself by a fourth French soldier. Dickson parried

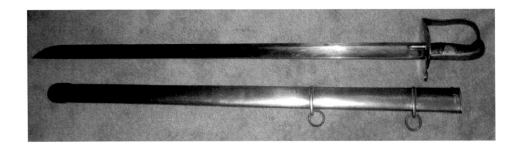

Heavy Cavalry Sword, 1796, similar to that used by the Scots Greys at Waterloo.
The actual sword wielded to good effect by Sergeant Charles Ewart is to be found in the National Museum of

Sergeant Ewart capturing the Eagle of the 45th French Regiment. It is interesting to note that the Scots Greys have moustaches, which were 'fashionable' in the Regiment at the time.

Corporal Dickson wearing his Waterloo Medal and his Long Service and Good Conduct Medal

the bayonet thrust, allowing Ewart to cut down the Eagle bearer. Armour secured the position by putting the remaining man to the sword. General Ponsonby then ordered Ewart to take his prize to Brussels.

Dickson continued to charge, spurred on by the enthusiasm of Lieutenant Colonel Hamilton, and eventually reached the French guns and put 15 of them out of action. ' We sabred the gunners, lamed the horses and cut their traces and harnesses'. An escape from the French Lancers was made possible by the intervention of the 16th Light Dragoons. To complete Dickson's day, his wounded horse Rattler, whom he had reluctantly left behind, made its own way back to the British lines. Although not officially recorded as wounded, Dickson states that he received only two slight wounds, one from a bayonet and the other from a lance.

Dickson replaced Ewart as Troop Sergeant Major, when the latter left the Scots Greys to become an Ensign in the 5th Veteran Battalion.

Served 31 years with the Regiment and therefore received a Long Service & Good Conduct Medal. Discharged through Chelsea Pension office, 1837, due to rheumatism of the shoulders and pain in his side following an injury sustained in his right side, 15th February 1830, whilst in Cloghean, Ireland, when his horse fell upon him whilst on duty. His general conduct is described as exemplary by Lieutenant Colonel Charles Wyndham. Joined the Fife Light Horse. Resided, Crail.

Died, 6 Philbrick Terrace, Nunhead Lane , Surrey, 16 July 1880, age 90. Death certificate says Army Pensioner; death due to 'Failure of heart's action and decay of nature'. His son, W.A. Dickson, also of 6 Philbrick Terrace, was present at his death. He was the longest survivor of all the men who charged at Waterloo.

Waterloo Medal extant, National War Museum Scotland.

Corporal James HARPER

Born, Kilmarnock; a labourer by trade. Killed in action at Waterloo.

Corporal Samuel TAR

Born, Biggleswade, Bedfordshire; a labourer by trade. Enlistment height, 5ft 7ins. Wounded by lances at Waterloo in the left foot and leg, also between the shoulders (witnessed by Lieutenant Gape, and described in his letter home). Dickson says that Tar was seen falling wounded from his horse. Reduced to Private, September 1815. Served about 20 years with the Regiment.

Waterloo Medal extant (Provenance: Buckland Dix & Wood 1994).

Corporal Alexander WILSON

Born, Libberton, Edinburgh; a labourer by trade. Enlistment height, 6ft 4ins. Served 19 years with the Regiment. Appears not to have sustained any injuries at Waterloo. Discharged through Chelsea Pension office, August 1818, due to scrofulous and chronic rheumatism. His general conduct was described as very good.

Waterloo Medal extant (Provenance: Sotheby 1995).

Trumpeter Joseph REEVES*

Born, St Martins, Worcester; a labourer by trade. Enlisted, 1804; height, 5ft 8ins. Charged at Waterloo with Sergeant Ewart and mentioned in Corporal Dickson's account of the battle. Appears not to have sustained any injuries at Waterloo. Served 27 years with the Regiment. Discharged through Chelsea Pension office, 1829, due to being worn out. His general conduct was described as good.

Private John ATHERLEY*

Born, Stanton, Nottingham; a labourer by trade. Enlisted, May 1813; height, 5ft 10ins. Appears not to have sustained any injuries at Waterloo. Served 24 years with the Regiment. Discharged through Chelsea Pension office, October 1835, due to disability and injury received in service. His general conduct was described as good.

Waterloo Medal extant (Provenance: Glendining 1922).

Private John BROBIN

Enlisted, March 1809. Appears not to have sustained any injuries at Waterloo.

Private Francis BROWN

Enlisted, May 1811; a slater by trade. Enlistment height, 5ft 10ins. Injured his hip when he fell off his horse when it was killed at Waterloo. Discharged through Kilmainham Pension office, November 1818.

Waterloo Medal extant (Provenance: Glendining 1964).

Private James BROWN

Born, 1790. Enlisted, 2nd October 1805. Appears not to have sustained any injuries at Waterloo. Died, 1840; buried near Asheville, North Carolina, U.S.A. (*Eagle and Carbine*, Vol 14, 1985, page 220).

Private George BUTLER

Born, Castleton; a labourer by trade. Wounded at Waterloo, suffering lance wounds to the head, loins and right hand; subsequently died from the wounds.

Waterloo Medal extant (Provenance: Dix Noonan Webb 2004).

Private John COLLIER*

Born, Panckem, Hereford; a stonemason by trade. Enlisted, 12th January 1804; height, 6ft 3ins. Appears not to have sustained any injuries at Waterloo. Served 24 years with the Regiment. Discharged through Chelsea Pension office, 1826, due to being worn out. His general conduct was described as being very good.

Waterloo Medal extant (Provenance: Glendining 1970, Allison collection).

Private Adam COLQUHOUN

Appears not to have sustained any injuries at Waterloo. Reported dead by Lieutenant Colonel Clarke, 11th April 1816. His Waterloo Medal 1815 was sent to his father in Dumbartonshire, 8th November 1817.

Waterloo Medal extant, Regimental Museum.

Private Robert CRAIG

Born, Paisley; a weaver by trade. Enlistment height, 5ft 10ins. Wounded three times at Waterloo, suffering a lance wound to the right breast, a sabre wound to the forehead, and a bayonet wound to the back of the neck. Served nine years with the Regiment. Discharged through Kilmainham Pension office, June 1826.

Private William CRAIG

Born, Paisley; a labourer by trade. Killed in action at Waterloo.

Private John DALZIEL

Enlisted, August 1806. Appears not to have sustained any injuries at Waterloo.

Private William DUNLOP

Enlisted, May 1814. Wounded at Waterloo and sent to Brussels to recover.

Private John DUNN*

Born, New Mills, Ayr; a weaver by trade. Enlisted, December 1793; height, 5ft 9ins. Appears not to have sustained any injuries at Waterloo. Served 26 years with the Regiment. Discharged, 1818, due to being worn out through length of service. His general conduct was described as good.

 Waterloo Medal extant (Provenance: Lockdales 2009).

Private George ELLINGWORTH

Born, Brotherton, Selby, Yorkshire; a labourer by trade. Killed in action at Waterloo.

Private John GILLIES

Born, Humbie, co Haddington; a labourer by trade. Appears not to have sustained any injuries at Waterloo.

Private William GORDON*

Born, Kinghorn, Fife; a labourer by trade. Enlistment height, 5ft 9ins. Appears not to have sustained any injuries at Waterloo. Served 28 years with the Regiment. Discharged due to being worn out. His general conduct was described as good.

Private Robert GOURLEY

Enlisted, March 1807. Appears not to have sustained any injuries at Waterloo.

 Waterloo Medal extant (Provenance: Spink 1979).

Private Robert GREIG

Enlisted, October 1806. Appears not to have sustained any injuries at Waterloo.

Private John HALL

Born, Cambletown; a labourer by trade. Killed in action at Waterloo.

Private John HARKNESS

Born, Galston, Ayr; a stockingmaker by trade. Wounded at Waterloo, suffering a severe musket shot to the left foot. Sent to Brussels to recover.

Private John HENDERSON*

Born, Northumberland; a shoemaker by trade. Enlisted, 1805, age 18. Severely wounded at Waterloo; sent to Brussels to recover; returned to England, 8th July 1815. Served 12 years with the Regiment. Joined the 5th Royal Veteran Battalion, served only 55 days. Discharged through Chelsea Pension Office, 18th January 1816, due to severe wounds rendering him unfit for further service Described as a shoemaker living in Hounslet, Leeds, April 1816.

Private Henry HODKINSON

Enlisted, September 1812. Wounded at Waterloo.

Private William JONES

Born, Westbourn, Hampshire; a farrier by trade. Enlisted, May 1805; height, 5ft 7ins. Appears not to have sustained any injuries at Waterloo. Served 24 years with the Regiment. Discharged through Chelsea Pension office, 1827, due to being worn out. His general conduct was described as good.

Private Samuel KENMUIR

Born, Kilmarnock; a weaver by trade. Died of wounds sustained at Waterloo, 24th September 1815, after being transferred to Brussels. His agent received 11s 10d, 14th February 1816.

Private James KING

Born, Burbridge, Wiltshire. Enlisted, 28th January 1804. Part of the Cavalry on duty with the Staff Corps. Reported dead by Lieutenant Colonel Clarke, 11th April 1816.

Private John LANE (LAND)*

Born, West Harnham, Salisbury; a labourer by trade. Enlisted, May 1801; height, 5ft 8ins. Appears not to have sustained any injuries at Waterloo. Served 22 years with the Regiment. Discharged through Chelsea Pension office, 1821, due to being unfit for service because of chronic rheumatism. His general conduct was described as very good.

Waterloo Medal extant (Provenance: Christie 1965).

Private James LIDDLE

Born, Airdrie; a weaver by trade. Enlisted, May 1801. Taken prisoner by the French at Waterloo; released from French prison, September 1815; originally reported as killed in action.

Private James LOVE
Born, Dalsey; a mason by trade. Killed in action at Waterloo.

Private Robert LYLE
Born, Killochan, Ayrshire; a labourer by trade. Killed in action at Waterloo.

Private James LYON
Enlisted, 23rd August 1806, Glasgow. Died of wounds sustained at Waterloo

Private William M'NAIR*
Born, New Monkland, Lanark; a weaver by trade. Served East Lothian Fencible Cavalry, 13th October 1796–March 1800. Enlisted, March 1800; height, 5ft 8ins. Appears not to have sustained any injuries at Waterloo. Served 17 years with the Regiment (total service 25 years). Discharged through Chelsea Pension office, 1818. His general conduct was described as very good.

Private Alexander MacKAY
Born, Glasgow; a tinsmith by trade. Killed in action at Waterloo.

Private William MacKIE
Born, Glasgow; a labourer by trade. Died of wounds sustained at Waterloo.

Private David McALL
Born, Fauls, Shropshire; a labourer by trade. Died, Yarmouth Hospital, July 1816, from wounds sustained at Waterloo.. His agent received 13s 5d.

Private John McCULLOCH
Born, Kilmarnock; a labourer by trade. Killed in action at Waterloo.

Private John McGEE
Enlisted, Glasgow, 17th December 1811. Wounded at Waterloo; sent to Brussels to recover. Mentioned in Corporal Dickson's Memoirs (Low, 1911).

Private John MATTHEWS
Enlisted, 15th June 1811. Wounded at Waterloo; appears to have recovered from his wound.

Private William MILLAR
Born, Egham, Surrey; a labourer by trade. Killed in action at Waterloo.

Private James MONTGOMERY
Enlisted, March 1813. Appears not to have sustained any injuries at Waterloo.

Private John MOORE*

Born, Ayr; a labourer by trade. Enlisted, 1805; height, 5ft 6ins. Appears not to have sustained any injuries at Waterloo. Served 13 years with the Regiment. Discharged through Chelsea Pension Office, 1817, due to general debility and diseased testicles. His general conduct was described as extremely good, exemplary.

Private William MURDOCH

Born, Auchinleck, East Ayrshire; a labourer by trade. Died from wounds sustained at Waterloo, Brussels, 6th July 1815.

Private William PARK

Born, Perth. Served, Perth Fencibles, 1st November 1799–7th April 1800. Enlisted, June 1800. Appears not to have sustained any injuries at Waterloo.

Private William PATTON* (1)

Born, Kilbarchan, Renfrew; a weaver by trade. Enlisted, October 1799; height, 5ft 8ins. Appears not to have sustained any injuries at Waterloo. Later injured left side due to a fall from his horse when travelling from Canterbury to Carlisle. Served 20 years with the Regiment. Discharged through Chelsea Pension office, 1817, due to injuries sustained from the fall. His general conduct was described as extremely good.

Private William PATTON (2)

Born, Tillicultrie, Clackmannanshire; a mason by trade. Appears not to have sustained any injuries at Waterloo.

Private Robert REID*

Born, Galston, Ayr; a nailer by trade. Enlisted, November 1805; height, 5ft 6ins. Appears not to have sustained any injuries at Waterloo. Served 16 years with the Regiment. Discharged through Chelsea Pension office, 1826, being unfit due to gonorrhoea and syphilis followed by inflammation of the periosteum of the cranium. His general conduct was described as very good.

Private William ROSS*

Born, Libberton, Edinburgh; a labourer by trade. Enlisted, July 1805; height, 5ft 8ins. Appears not to have sustained any injuries at Waterloo. Served 18 years with the Regiment. Discharged through the Chelsea Pension office, 1821, due to being unfit as a consequence of chronic rheumatism. His general conduct was described as very good.

Private James SMITH

Born, Norton Lees, Yorkshire; a labourer by trade. Enlisted, November 1806. Appears not to have sustained any injuries at Waterloo. At Brussels after Waterloo.

Private William SMITH
Born, Ashburn. Enlisted, 1799. Appears not to have sustained any injuries at Waterloo.

Private William STORRIE
Born, Renfrew; a carpenter by trade. Enlisted, July 1803. Taken prisoner by the French at Waterloo; released from French prison, 18th September 1815; originally reported as killed in action.
   Waterloo Medal extant, Regimental Museum.

Private William SUTHERLAND
Born, Cambuslang, Lanarkshire; a weaver by trade. Killed in action at Waterloo.

Private William SYKES*
Born, Brompton, Huntingdon; a labourer by trade. Enlisted, March 1806; height, 5ft 10ins. Corporal, 1818; Sergeant, October 1824. Appears not to have sustained any injuries at Waterloo. Served 33 years with the Regiment. Discharged through Chelsea Pension office, July 1837, unfit due to dyspnoea (breathlessness) and chronic rheumatism. He was described as an unexceptional soldier.
   Waterloo Medal extant, Regimental Museum.

Private Thomas TAYLOR
Born, Fordingbridge, Hampshire; a weaver by trade. Killed in action at Waterloo.

Private Ebenezer THOMPSON*
Born, Falkirk, Stirling; a stocking maker by trade. Enlisted, 1797; height, 5ft 8ins. Appears not to have sustained any injuries at Waterloo. Served 22 years with the Regiment. Discharged through Chelsea Pension office, August 1817, due to a double rupture and being worn out. His general conduct was described as extremely good.
   Returned to Back Row (now Manor Street), Falkirk; had 2 sons; described in 1841 Census as a pensioner.

Private George TURNER
Born, Yetholm, Kelso; a baker by trade. Killed in action at Waterloo.

Private John TURNER
Born, Alnwick, Northumberland. Killed in action at Waterloo.

Private John VEAZEY
Enlisted, June 1803. Appears not to have sustained any injuries at Waterloo.

Private Robert WALLACE*
Born, Clackmannan; a labourer by trade. Enlisted, June 1808, Edinburgh, age 19; height, 6ft. Private, 7 years; Corporal, 7 years; Sergeant, 8 years; later Troop Sergeant Major. Appears not to have sustained

any injuries at Waterloo. Served 24 years with the Regiment. Discharged through Chelsea Pension office, Brighton, April 1831. His general conduct was described as particularly good. Messenger, Queen's Body Guard, 1872. Died, 1874, after 50 years service in uniform.

Private Thomas WATSON

Enlisted, September 1812. Wounded at Waterloo. Sent to England, 8th July. Transferred to 5th Royal Veteran Battalion (Lieutenant Colonel Clarke, April 1816).

Private Richard WHAREM

Born, Barnsley, Yorkshire: a blacksmith by trade. Enlistment height, 5ft 10ins. Appears not to have sustained any injuries at Waterloo. Served ten years with the Regiment. Discharged, 1822. Late pension claim, age 78, 1871; received 9d per day.

Private John WISE* (WYSE)

Born, Falkirk, Stirling; a labourer by trade. Surname sometimes spelt Wyse. Enlisted, 1806; height, 5ft 8ins. Appears not to have sustained any injuries at Waterloo. Served 24 years with the Regiment. Discharged, 1827, due to being worn out. His general conduct was described as good. Returned to Stirlingshire, lived in Canal Street, Grangemouth. On the 1841 census, described as a man of independent means, age 50 years. One of the celebrated Falkirk 13.

Private Peter WOTHERSPOON

Born, Abernethy, Perthshire; a labourer by trade. Killed in action at Waterloo.

Private Robert YOUNG

Born, Paisley; a labourer by trade. Died of wounds sustained at Waterloo, 29th June 1815.

Fenton's Troop

Captain Thomas Charles FENTON

Born, 1790. Son of James Fenton, Loversall. Served in the Peninsula with 4th Light Dragoons, age 19. Transferred to the Scots Greys, age 25. Letters he wrote to his parents between 1809-1816 (*Journal of Army Historical Research*, 1975: 216) confirm he was at the battles of Talavera and Salamanca and he describes narrowly escaping injury from a cannon ball. Another letter verifies that he commanded a Troop at Waterloo when 19 of his men were killed in action and 22 were wounded. Additionally he laments the tragic death of his Brigade Commander, General Ponsonby. Fenton was one of only a few officers in the Greys who had had combat experience prior to Waterloo.

Left the Regiment, 1819. Died, 6th February 1841, Tidenham, a district of Chepstow, where he lived. His death certificate gives the cause of death as inflammatory fever (most likely an infection of unknown origin) and describes him as a Gentleman, age 51. Due to death, not eligible to claim the Military General Service Medal 1793-1814, for his Peninsula service.

Waterloo Medal extant, Regimental Museum.

Lieutenant James Reginald Torin GRAHAM

Son of James Graham, Esq., Barrack Lodge and Rickerby, Cumberland. Joined Scots Greys, 1814, age 15. Captain, 1820; Major, 1837. After the battle of Waterloo, he was in charge of the burial of the men from the Greys, including Cornet Shuldham. Died, 1865, age 66, in Kensington; buried, Brompton Cemetery.

Waterloo Medal extant, Border Regiment Museum.

Troop Sergeant Major John WEIR

Born, Mauchline; a shoemaker by trade. Joined the Greys, 1798. Killed at Waterloo, the only Troop Sergeant Major to be so. His name was written in blood on his forehead, so his body could be identified and as proof he had not absconded with the troop's money which was in his charge.

Sergeant James ANDREW*

Born, Glasgow; a shoemaker by trade. Enlisted, 1796; height, 5ft 1in. Appears not to have sustained any injuries at Waterloo. Damaged his back in a riding accident whilst at Riding School. Served 27 years with the Regiment. Discharged through Chelsea Pension office, 1821. His general conduct was described as good.

Sergeant Richard HAYWARD

Born, Milton Hants. Severely wounded at Waterloo; at Brussels, September 1815, recovering from his wounds. Served 14 years with the Regiment. Joined, 5th Veteran Battalion, 24th January 1816.

Waterloo Medal extant, private collection (Provenance: Richard Kirch 1993).

Captain Thomas Charles Fenton

CERTIFIED COPY OF AN ENTRY OF DEATH
COPI DILYS O GOFNOD MARWOLAETH

Given at the GENERAL REGISTER OFFICE
Fe'i rhoddwyd yn y GENERAL REGISTER OFFICE

Application Number } 914487-1
Rhif y cais

REGISTRATION DISTRICT
DOSBARTH COFRESTRU } OF CHEPSTOW

DEATH in the Sub district of
MARWOLAETH yn Is-ddosbarth } Chepstow

in the Counties of Monmouth and Gloucester
yn

1841

Columns: Colofnau: No. Rhif	When and where died Pryd a lle y bu farw	Name and surname Enw a chyfenw	Sex Rhyw	Age Oed	Occupation Gwaith	Cause of death Achos marwolaeth	Signature, description and residence of informant Llofnod, disgrifiad a chyfeiriad yr hysbysydd	When registered Pryd y cofrestrwyd	Signature of registrar Llofnod y cofrestrydd

CERTIFIED to be a true copy of an entry in the certified copy of a Register of Deaths in the District above mentioned.
TYSTIOLAETHWYD ei fod yn gopi cywir o gofnod mewn copi y tystiwyd iddo o Gofrestr Marwolaethau yn y Dosbarth a enwyd uchod.

Given at the GENERAL REGISTER OFFICE, under the Seal of the said Office.
Fe'i rhoddwyd yn y GENERAL REGISTER OFFICE, o dan Sêl y swyddfa a enwyd.

the .... day of .... February .... } 2009
y .... dydd o fis ....

WARNING: THERE ARE OFFENCES RELATING TO FALSIFYING OR ALTERING A CERTIFICATE AND USING OR POSSESSING A FALSE CERTIFICATE © CROWN COPYRIGHT
RHYBUDD: MAE YNA DROSEDDAU YN YMWNEUD Â FFUGIO NEU ADDASU TYSTYSGRIF NEU DDEFNYDDIO TYSTYSGRIF FFUG NEU WRTH FOD AG UN YN EICH MEDDIANT. © HAWLFRAINT Y GORON

WARNING: A CERTIFICATE IS NOT EVIDENCE OF IDENTITY.
RHYBUDD: NID YW TYSTYSGRIF YN PROFI PWY YDYCH CHI.

1069865 17744 07/07 3MSPSL 010546

WDXZ 132742

See note overleaf
Gweler trosodd

MS

Fenton's Death Certificate

Fenton's Gravestone in Chepstow

The Waterloo Medals 1815 to the Swan Brothers.
The lower slide bar on William's medal (left) is inscribed with a dedication to his younger brother, Peter,
who was wounded at Waterloo

Sergeant Thomas SOARS

At Waterloo, wounded in the left ear, causing deafness, and sustained a severely injured left thigh. Served 25 years with the Regiment; 15 years as Sergeant.

Waterloo Medal extant, Regimental Museum.

Sergeant William SWAN

Elder of the two Swan brothers (see later: Private Peter Swan, page 108). Enlisted, June 1799. Corporal, February, 1810; Sergeant, 1812; Troop Sergeant Major, 1812; Regimental Sergeant Major, 1821. Died, 1825; succeeded as Regimental Sergeant Major by younger brother, Peter. Appears not to have sustained any injuries at Waterloo.

Waterloo Medal extant, author's collection.

Corporal John CRAIG

Enlisted, 1800. At Waterloo, sustained a sabre cut in the head and hand, also bayonet wounds in his loins and a contusion of his left shoulder. At Brussels, September 1815, recovering from his wounds.

Waterloo Medal extant.

Corporal Thomas DAVIS (DAVIES)

Enlisted, May 1799. Surname also given as Davies. Appears not to have sustained any injuries at Waterloo.

Corporal John MAIN* (MAIR)

Born, Worcester; a labourer by trade. Surname also given as Mair. Enlisted, 1803; height, 5ft 11ins. Served eleven years as Private; two years as Corporal; ten years as Sergeant. Severely wounded and taken prisoner at Waterloo (originally thought to have been killed). In a French prison until September 1815. Served 24 years with the Regiment. Discharged through Chelsea Pension office, April 1826, due to being worn out. His general conduct was described as very good.

Corporal Robert THOMPSON*

Born, Blantyre, Lanark; a labourer by trade. Enlisted, 1803; height, 6ft. Corporal, 25th April 1815; reduced to Private, November 1815. Appears not to have sustained any injuries at Waterloo. Served 24 years with the Regiment. Discharged through Chelsea Pension office, October 1826, due to being worn out. His general conduct was described as very good.

Waterloo Medal extant (Provenance: Dix Noonan Webb 2010).

Trumpeter Henry BOWIG

Enlisted, 1805. Also a Trumpeter in Cathcart's and Baird's Troops before joining Fenton's Troop. Reported sick in Brussels in September 1815. Served in excess of ten years with the Regiment. Residing in Manchester, April 1816.

Private Thomas ANDERSON*

Born, Dalkeith, Edinburgh; a candlemaker by trade. Enlisted, April 1793. Appears not to have sustained any injuries at Waterloo. Served 25 years with the Regiment. Discharged through Chelsea Pension office, October 1816, due to chronic rheumatism. His general conduct was described as very good.

Private John ARKLIE

Enlisted, April 1813; a gardener by trade. Enlistment height, 5ft 8ins. Appears not to have sustained any injuries at Waterloo. Discharged through Kilmainham Pension office. He was recorded as being subject to scrofulous of the glands and of general bad habit of the body.

Private James ARMOUR

Born, Edinburgh; a labourer by trade. Enlisted, 1807; height, 5ft 11ins. Sustained a fractured clavicle from being thrown from his horse. Wounded at Waterloo, where he displayed gallantry, included severe lance wounds in the loins and two wounds to the right knee. At Brussels, September 1815, recovering from his wounds. Discharged through Chelsea Pension office, 1816, due to injuries sustained when he was thrown from his horse whilst on duty in Brussels, July 1815, having recovered from the wounds he received at Waterloo. Described by Lieutenant Colonel Clarke as 'A man of good character'.

Private John ARTHUR

Born, Cumbernauld, Lanarkshire; a wright by trade. Killed in action at Waterloo.

Private William BALLANTYNE*

Born, Barony, Glasgow; a flax dresser by trade. Enlisted, March 1811; height, 5ft 9ins. Appears not to have sustained any injuries at Waterloo. Promoted Corporal, 1818. Sustained a double rupture when he fell from his horse. Served 12 years with the Regiment. Discharged through Chelsea Pension office, 1821.

Waterloo Medal extant, private collection.

Private George BIDDOLPH (BIDDLE)

Enlisted, June 1813, age 18. His surname is also given as Biddle. Appears not to have sustained any injuries at Waterloo. Present on command in Brussels, attending the wounded horses.

Private Alexander BLACKADDER

Enlisted, July 1806. Appears not to have sustained any injuries at Waterloo. Present on command in Brussels, attending the wounded horses.

Private Samuel BOULTER

Enlisted, December, 1805. Appears not to have sustained any injuries at Waterloo. In a letter to his brother, William, in Stowmarket, Suffolk, Boulter describes the post-Waterloo carnage and says how 'affecting' it was to see so many men lying dead and a great many wounded calling for water. He says that there were many men with multiple wounds, some with their legs hanging off. According to

Boulter, almost everyone who underwent amputation did not survive (this may have been a rather sweeping observation as it is not supported by other accounts, see Crumplin, 2007, who gives a 31% mortality rate for all limb amputations). Boulter concludes by stating 'we buried all of ours that was Dead'.

Waterloo Medal extant (Provenance: Glendining 1977).

Private Cunningham BOWES*

From Paisley, Renfrew; a farmer by trade. Enlisted, 1811; height, 5ft 9ins. Wounded at Waterloo, sustaining a sabre wound to the left hand. Served 19 years with the Regiment. Discharged through Chelsea Pension office, May 1829, due to hepatic (liver) disease and being worn out. His general conduct was described as good.

Waterloo Medal extant, private collection.

Private Stephen BROOKES*

Born, Hinckley, Leicestershire; a stocking maker by trade. Enlisted, 1798; height, 5ft 10ins. Served 20 years with the Regiment. Sustained lance wounds to the left side and right breast at Waterloo. Discharged through Chelsea Pension office, 1816.

Waterloo Medal extant (Provenance: Mackenzie collection 1934).

Private Adam BROWN*

Born, Kilmarnock; a weaver by trade. Enlisted, 1803, age 17; height, 5ft 9ins. Served 15 years with the Regiment. Wounded in the head and sustained lance wounds on the right side and upper right arm at Waterloo. Promoted Corporal, age 32. Discharged through Chelsea Pension office, 1817. His general conduct was described as extremely good and he is recorded as having displayed great gallantry at Waterloo.

Private Samuel BROWN

Born, Nuttsford (probably Knutsford, Cheshire); a weaver by trade. Killed in action at Waterloo.

Private Thomas BROWN

Born, Alnwick, Northumberland; a blacksmith by trade. Killed in action at Waterloo.

Private James BRYCE (BRUCE)

Enlisted, November 1812, age 24 years. His surname is also given as Bruce. Killed in action at Waterloo.

Private William BRYCE

Born, Bo'ness, Firth of Forth; a collier by trade. Killed in action at Waterloo.

Private John CAMPBELL

Born, Stevenstone, Ayr. Enlistment height, 5ft 9ins. Appears not to have sustained any injuries at Waterloo. Served 28 years with the Regiment.

Private John CLARKE*

Born, Canterbury, Kent; a labourer by trade. Enlisted, January 1804. Wounded at Waterloo with two sabre cuts to the left knee. At Brussels, September 1815, recovering from his wounds. Served 24 years with the Regiment. Discharged, October 1826, due to being worn out. His general conduct was described as very good.

Waterloo Medal extant (Provenance: Bonhams 2007).

Private Robert CURRIE

Enlisted, December 1806. Appears not to have sustained any injuries at Waterloo. After Waterloo, he was on duty at Brussels.

Waterloo Medal extant (Provenance: Spink 1950).

Private Joshua DAWSON

Born, Otley, Yorkshire; a butcher by trade. Enlisted, October 1812. Killed in action at Waterloo.

Private William DICK*

Born, Paisley, Renfrew; a weaver by trade. Served Lanark Fencible Cavalry 10th March 1798–9th March 1800. Enlisted, 10th March 1800; height, 5ft 9in. Wounded in back by a lance and lost his left eye to a musket shot at Waterloo. Served 22 years with the Regiment. Discharged through Chelsea Pension office, August 1818, as a consequence of severe wounds received at Waterloo. His general conduct was described as good.

Private John DOBBIE

Born, Glasgow. Enlistment height, 5ft 7in. Wounded by musket shot in the right leg at Waterloo. Served 23 years with the Regiment.

Private John FERGUSON*

Born, Paisley, Renfrew; a labourer by trade. Enlisted, October 1799; height, 5ft 9in. Wounded in the left arm by a lance at Waterloo. Served 24 years with the Regiment. Discharged through Chelsea Pension office, October 1821, due to rheumatism and damage to the left arm from a wound sustained at Waterloo. His general conduct was described as very good.

Private Duncan FORBES

Born, Inverie; a shoemaker by trade. Killed in action at Waterloo.

Private John GOULD*

Born, Edinburgh; a tailor by trade. Enlisted, 1808; height, 5ft 7in. Appears not to have sustained any injuries at Waterloo. Served 24 years with the Regiment. Discharged through Chelsea Pension office, 1830, at his own request. His general conduct was described as very good.

Private James GREEN

Enlisted, May 1812, age 18. Appears not to have sustained any injuries at Waterloo.

Private Thomas HARRIS

Born, Broughton, Scottish Borders; a labourer by trade. Died of wounds sustained at Waterloo, 2nd July 1815.

Private William HOWIE

Born, Kilwinning, Ayr; a mason by trade. Enlisted, May 1808; height, 5ft 9in. Served ten years with the Regiment. Badly wounded in the right arm at Waterloo. Discharged, October 1816, as unfit for service. He was described as a clean soldier.

Private Alexander HUNTER

Born, Borthwick, Edinburgh; a labourer by trade. Wounded at Waterloo. At Brussels, September 1815, recovering from his wounds.

Private Hugh HUNTER

Born, 20th June 1790. Enlisted, 6th August 1807, age 17. Appears not to have sustained any injuries at Waterloo.

Private Robert HUNTER*

Born, Kelso; a shoemaker by trade. Enlisted, 1805; height, 5ft 7ins. Appears not to have sustained any injuries at Waterloo. Served 12 years with the Regiment. Discharged through Chelsea Pension office, 1816, due to an affliction or bladder disease. He was described as a clean good man.

Private Archibald HUTTON*

Born, Falkirk. Enlisted, 1812; height, 6ft. At Waterloo, received a severe contusion of the right leg affecting the foreleg. Served 16 years with the Regiment. General conduct described as very good. Discharged through Chelsea Pension office, 1826, due inflammation of the lungs producing shortness of breath. He was one of the celebrated Falkirk 13.

Private James JONES*

Born, Poole, Dorset; a labourer by trade. Enlisted, March 1805; height, 5ft 9ins. Received severe lance wounds in the left side and a sabre cut on the hand at Waterloo. Served 15 years with the Regiment. Discharged through Chelsea Pension office, 1818, due to asthma. His general conduct was described as very good.

Private Archibald KEAN

Enlisted, January 1811. Appears not to have sustained any injuries at Waterloo.

Private Samuel KINDER

Enlisted, 1804. Appears not to have sustained any injuries at Waterloo.

Private George KITCHEN

Born, Broughton, Scottish Borders; a labourer by trade. Died of wounds sustained at Waterloo, 8 July 1815.

Private Andrew KNIGHT

Born, Inveresk, Musselburgh; a labourer by trade. Killed in action at Waterloo .

Private Samuel LAW

Enlisted, 1813, age 22. Died of wounds sustained at Waterloo.

Private John LIDDLE

Enlisted, 12th January 1799. Appears not to have sustained any injuries at Waterloo.
  Waterloo Medal extant, Regimental Museum.

Private Robert LITTLEJOHN

Appears not to have sustained any injuries at Waterloo. A letter from Lieutenant Colonel Clarke, April 1816, to Robert's father, Thomas Littlejohn, a tailor, High St, Hamilton, stated that Littlejohn had died (cause of death unknown). His Waterloo Medal was forwarded as an act of kindness and respect, 8th November 1817.

Private James McLAUCHLAN

Born, Sanquhar, Dumfries; a cotton spinner by trade. Killed in action at Waterloo.

Private Joseph MACRO

Enlisted, November 1805. Appears not to have sustained any injuries at Waterloo. After Waterloo, he was on duty at Chantilly.

Private Peter MILLER*

Born, Falkirk; a baker by trade. Enlisted, 1804, age 36; height, 5ft 9ins. Severely wounded at Waterloo by a musket ball to the right side. Served 15 years with the Regiment. Discharged through Chelsea Pension office, 1817, due to being worn out. His general conduct was described as extremely good. One of the celebrated Falkirk 13.

Private John MITCHELL (MITCHEL)
Born, 24ᵗʰ September 1789. His surname is also given as Mitchel. Enlisted, 2ⁿᵈ August 1805. At Brussels, September 1815, recovering from his wounds sustained at Waterloo.

Private William PEARSON
Born, 15ᵗʰ August 1788. Enlisted, 13ᵗʰ January 1805. Sustained severe lance wounds to right breast, the loins, right arm and right thigh at Waterloo. At Brussels, September 1815, recovering from his wounds.
   Waterloo Medal extant, Regimental Museum.

Private Luke PRIESTLEY
Born, Portsham, Weymouth; a labourer by trade. Killed in action at Waterloo.

Private James PYE
Born, Astley; a labourer by trade. Died of wounds sustained at Waterloo, 29ᵗʰ June 1815.

Private William REID
Enlisted, 15ᵗʰ October 1807. Wounded at Waterloo. At Brussels, September 1815, recovering from his wounds.

Private David ROLLAND
Born, Strathblane, Glasgow; a mason by trade. Killed in action at Waterloo

Private John ROSS*
Born, Berwick; a labourer by trade. Enlisted, August 1805; height, 5ft 7ins. Injured by a fall from his horse. Appears not to have sustained any injuries at Waterloo. Served 17 years with the Regiment. Discharged, August 1821, due to being unfit. His general conduct was described as good, except that he deserted on one occasion.

Private William ROWATT
Born, Kirkintilloch, Dunbarton; a labourer by trade. Died of wounds sustained at Waterloo, 2 July 1815.

Private John SENIOR
Born, Emley, Yorkshire; a blacksmith by trade. Killed in action at Waterloo.

Private John SIMMONS
Born, Bunbury (Burnbury); a labourer by trade. Killed in action at Waterloo.

Private William SMITH
Born, Ashburn; a blacksmith by trade. Enlistment height, 5ft 9ins. Appears not to have sustained any injuries at Waterloo.

Private David STODDART
Born, Newbattle, Tyne & Wear; a labourer by trade. Killed in action at Waterloo.

Private Peter SWAN*
Born, Renfrew; a weaver by trade. Enlisted, October 1805; height, 5ft 11ins. Served ten years as Private; seven years as Corporal; seven years as Sergeant, 24th July 1823–1st October 1830. At Waterloo, sustained lance wounds to the right hand with dislocation of the thumb and a lance wound in the right knee. In 1862, Swan gave an account of the capture of the Eagle of the 45th French Regiment (published in *The Times*). I Sworn on oath, he states that the Eagle was initially seized by Trumpeter Hutchinson who was immediately killed. Charles Ewart then fought to retake the prize., though the actual fight for the standard was not witnessed by Swan as he was engaged with the enemy. Served 27 years in the Regiment. Discharged through Chelsea Pension office, October 1830. His general conduct was described as good.
Waterloo Medal extant, author's collection.

Private Jonathan TAYLOR*
Born, Rotherham, Yorkshire, a ironcaster by trade. Enlisted, June 1804; height, 5ft 8ins. Appears not to have sustained any injuries at Waterloo. Served 24 years with the Regiment. Discharged through Chelsea Pension office, October 1826, due to being worn out. His general conduct was described as very good.
Waterloo Medal extant (Provenance: Dix Noonan Webb 2005).

Private Andrew THOMPSON*
Born, Sanguhar, Dumfries; a labourer by trade. Enlistment height, 5ft 9ins. Appears not to have sustained any injuries at Waterloo. Sustained chest injuries after his horse fell on him. Served 26 years with the Regiment. Discharged, 1821, due to spitting up blood and breathing difficulties. He was described as a clean active soldier.

Private Alexander WALKER
Born, Tengle; a labourer by trade. Killed in action at Waterloo.

Private John WATSON
Born, Glenholm, Peebles. Wounded in right leg and arm at Waterloo. Served 25 years with the Regiment.
Waterloo Medal extant.

Private Thomas WILMOT*
Born, Loughborough, Leicestershire; a blacksmith by trade. Enlisted, May 1799; height, 5ft 7ins. Appears not to have sustained any injuries at Waterloo. On duty Brussels, September 1815. Served 26 years with the Regiment. Discharged through Chelsea Pension office, 1823, due to being worn out because of his service. His general conduct was described as good.
Waterloo Medal extant (Provenance: Glendining 1990).

Scots Grey Officer in uniform, about 1815.

Published Sources

Almack, Edward (1908) *The History of the Second Dragoons*. London.

Cannon, Richard (1804) *Historical Record of the Royal Regiment of Scots Dragoons or Royal North British Dragoons*. London: Longman, Orme & Co.

Carlisle, Nicholas (1839) *Concise Account of Foreign Orders & Knighthoods Conferred on British Subjects*. (Reprinted 1992, Naval & Military Press)

Crumplin, Michael (2007) *Men of Steel*. Shrewsbury: Quiller Press.

Dalton, Charles (1978) *The Waterloo Roll Call*. Guildford: Arms & Armour Press.

Glover, Gareth (2004) *Letters from the Battle Of Waterloo*. Worcester: Greenhill Books.

Groves, Lieutenant Percy (1893) *Illustrated Histories of the Scottish Regiments, Book 2, 2nd Dragoons, Royal Scots Greys*. Edinburgh & London: W and AK Johnston.

Lagden, Alan and Sly, John (1998) *The 2/73rd at Waterloo*. Brightlingsea, Essex: Private Publication.

Low, Edward Bruce (1911) *With Napoleon at Waterloo*. London: Francis Griffiths.

Mollo, John (1973) *Waterloo Uniforms 1. British Cavalry*. London: Stanwill Press Ltd.

Mullen, A.L.T. (1990) *The Military General Service Medal Roll 1793-1814*. London: London Stamp Exchange.

Purves, Alec A. (1967) *Collecting Medals and Decorations*. London: Seaby.

Siborne, H.T. (1891) *Waterloo Letters*. (Reprinted 1993, Greenhill Books)

Wood, Stephen (1988) *In the Finest Tradition*. Somerset: Mainstream Publishing.

Periodicals

Journal of the Falkirk Local History Society (refs. Love; Kincaid)

Journal of the Society for Army Historical Research, 1959 (XXXVII, 152), 1979 (LIII, 216).

Regimental Magazine (Scots Greys), 1933 (ref. Charles Wyndham Memoir)

Manuscript Sources

NATIONAL ARCHIVES

WO12/517-522: Musters Rolls, 2nd Dragoons

WO 25: Casualty Returns (Registers, various)

WO31 Commander in Chief's Memoranda Papers

WO 97: Soldiers' Discharge Documents

WO 100/14: Waterloo Medal Roll

WO 116: Waterloo, Late Claims to Pension
WO 118: Examinations of Invalid Soldiers at Kilmainham
WO 120: Chelsea Outpensions Regimental Registers
MINT 16/112: Royal Mint Medal Roll for Waterloo

Various Private Letters, including letter from Cheney to his wife Elizabeth.

Index to Biographical Notes on the Officers and Men
Who Served with the Scots Greys at Waterloo